Magic Mobile

Michael Frayn was born in London in 1933 and began his career as a journalist on the *Guardian* and the *Observer*. His novels include *Towards the End of the Morning, Headlong, Spies* and *Skios*. His seventeen plays range from *Noises Off*, recently chosen as one of the nation's three favourite plays, to *Copenhagen*, which won the 1998 *Evening Standard* Award for Best Play of the Year and the 2000 Tony Award for Best Play. He is married to the writer Claire Tomalin.

by the same author

MAGIC
MOBILE

35 pre-loaded new text files by
MICHAEL FRAYN

First published in the UK and the USA in 2020
by Faber & Faber Limited
Bloomsbury House
74–77 Great Russell Street
London wc1b 3da

Typeset by Faber & Faber Limited
Printed and bound by CPI Group (UK) Ltd, Croydon, cr0 4yy

A CIP record for this book
is available from the British Library

isbn 978–0–571–35500–6

2 4 6 8 10 9 7 5 3 1

CONTENTS

BILL OF WRITES

A selection from our exciting new-season range of How-to-Write courses!

Introductory: How to know whether you really do have a burning desire to communicate something to the world, and, if so, what it is. Includes hands-on practical suggestions for writing:
* a mildly erotic novel set in West Bromwich in 1879;
* a blackly comic cookbook that includes, among many other hilariously disturbing recipes, one for mouldy turnips marinated in diesel oil;
* the constitution of a small dictatorship;
* a 700-page family saga written with a spray-gun on the side of a motorway bridge.

The course is conducted by Jemima Treeborough, who has a degree in goldfish husbandry, and, as you can see from the accompanying photograph, long blonde hair that falls attractively over one eye.

Preliminary: How to actually get started! For the student who has already told all their friends and relations that they're writing a book! Includes:

* how to know whether to start writing your book today, or whether it might be better to put it off until tomorrow;
* how to make a false start, thinking anything's better than sitting there gazing out of the window, and anyway you can always rewrite it later;
* how to make up to thirty more false starts.

The course is taught by Howard Souping, an acknowledged expert, who has written the first pages of seventy-three novels. The picture of Howard on the right, which was the only one he could find, shows him looking slightly inebriated at a beer festival in Queensland.

Intermediate: How to survive having got started. For the student who has already completed page one of a book, and is considering going on to page two. Includes:
* how to put off even thinking about it through the time-honoured literary device of cleaning out the 'p's and 'b's on your typewriter, now that typewriters have been replaced by word processors;
* how to recognise that it's impossible to write page two because, even after all that agonising, you

really need to go back and rewrite page one yet
again;

* how to break it to all the friends and relations you
told you were writing a book that you're not.

*Your guide here is Lemona Strood, who completed
seven of our How-to-Write courses and actually wrote
the first paragraph of page two of her critical history
of Todhunter Road, Streatham, before she gave up.
Her brave smile in the accompanying photograph is
testimony to her unquenchable spirit in the face of
disaster.*

Advanced: Understanding the financial aspects of
authorship – specialist tuition in every aspect of the
subject. Includes:

* how to write a cheque. Practical tuition in
writing cheques in favour of NoHow Literary
Ltd, with special emphasis on the correct
spelling of the payee's name. Your tutor here
is C. D. Thumb, Head of Home Sales, NoHow
Literary Ltd;

* how to ensure there is enough money in your
account to cover the cheque. Sebastian Sponge,
a distinguished fraudster who ran through his
life savings doing How-to-Write courses, and
who has subsequently served a prison sentence

for obtaining money by false pretences, discusses various advanced techniques;

* how to cope if your cheque is nominated for a major literary award. Celia Wozzard, who has done the flower-arrangement for many such occasions, takes you through the big night, including practical guidance on how to convey the text of your acceptance speech to the lectern so that people can't see that you've written it in advance before you knew whether you were going to win or not;

* how to recycle the speech as a religious tract if by any chance it shouldn't be needed. Your tutor here is Willa Domble, who has herself written fifty-three acceptance speeches over the years and never needed any of them;

* how to write a How-to-Write course. C. J. Sprew, who looks a bit dull in the photograph but who can in fact be quite amusing if you get him on to the subject of chromosome abnormalities in fruit flies, suggests trying to recoup your losses by writing a How-to-Write course, which he believes may be the literary form of the future now that no one reads anything any more but everyone wants to write the things that no one wants to read.

**AS TRUE AS I'M
STANDING HERE**

– . . . Scene one, take seventeen.

– And . . . action!

What is truth? A question humankind has been asking since man first learnt to speak. I'm Timothy Tompkins, Reader in Situational Logic at the University of Stoke-on-Trent, and I have come here to Athens, the birthplace of philosophy—

– Sorry, we're getting a bit of aircraft noise again.

– OK – cut!

*

– Scene one, take eighteen.

– And . . . action!

What is truth? A question humankind has been asking ever since man first learnt to speak. I'm Timothy Tompkins—

– Another plane. I don't know who picked a location right under the flight path into Athens airport . . .

9

– Cut, cut, cut!

*

– Scene one, take nineteen.

– OK, Tim – before the next plane. And – action!

What is truth? A question humankind has been asking since man first spurned to leak . . . I'm so sorry. Probably not a good idea drinking all that raki last night . . .

– Cut!

*

– Scene one, take twenty.

– OK, Tim – deep breath. No pressure. Chloe's rung air traffic control – we've got three minutes before the next plane. So just relax and enjoy it! We're in Greece, the sun's shining! You're doing great! And whenever you're ready . . . Very gently now . . . Action!

What is truth? A question humankind has been asking since man first learnt to speak. I'm Timothy Tompkins, Reader in Situational Logic at the University of Stroke-on-Tent . . .

*– Keep running. We'll cut around it. 'I'm Timothy
Tompkins . . .' Action!*

I'm Timothy Tompkins, Reader in Shituational
Logic . . .

*– Keep running, keep running. Tim, listen, we'll
come back and try the beginning again later
when we've all settled down.*

It's that bloody hotel they've put us in! I was kept
awake all night by some kind of plumping in the
thumbing . . .

*– Never mind. Just go straight on with 'Is it really
true, for a start . . . ?'*

Is it really true, for a start, that I'm standing here on
my own in front of the Parthenon, as I appear to be?
In this film you're for once going to be told the truth,
the whole truth, at any rate about this one simple
question. For the first time ever in the history of
presented documentaries we are going to show you
not an edited selection of the film we're making, but
the whole thing – the totally unedited rushes.

So you already know what's usually the first bit of
the truth to hit the cutting-room floor – that there's
also someone here who holds up the clapperboard

in front of my face at the beginning of each take. She's the camera assistant, and, just to fill in a bit more of the truth, she's called Jennie.

But you know that somewhere around there's also an invisible figure who keeps worrying about aircraft noise. That's Lewis, the sound man. And you've heard another voice doing all that stuff about 'Cut!' and 'Action!' That's Bill, the director. There's also a cameraman, of course, who's called George, plus Chloe, the production assistant, Grace, the make-up girl, and Josie, George's girlfriend, who's just come along for the ride.

Never before have you been allowed to see the take where I get my turds in a wangle. Or the one where I dry completely, as I have now, and have to get Chloe to bring the script . . . Thanks, Chloe . . .

'Because I'm not just making this stuff up as I go along . . .' Yes, because I'm not just making this stuff up as I go along. I wrote it, and I did seventeen drafts of it, and I was also up all night trying to learn it with my head going round from all that raki, and it wasn't me who ordered the second bottle . . .

Though I don't know why I'm not allowed to have an autocue like other presenters. Or just say the first thing that comes into my head, like some of them do these days. 'Wow! This is incredible! I don't believe this! How cool is this! Like, totally awesome . . . !'

Sorry, only I've been standing here in the midday sun for twenty takes and I think I'm beginning to get sunstroke, and possibly also skin cancer . . .

So where was I? Oh, yes, truth. So what in fact *is* truth? A question humankind has been asking since take one, all those many takes ago.

To answer it I have come here to Athens to meet a local expert the researchers have found, and he's going to be looking anxiously out of his front door waiting for the cue, and then the director's going to say 'Action', so the local expert's going to close the front door and then open it again and to his surprise see me standing there, and I'm going to say 'Hi, Spiros!', only his name's Stavros, so he closes the door and then he opens it again, and he's just as surprised to see me standing there again as he was before. So surprised that he never notices I'm being followed by Jennie, Lewis, Bill, George, Chloe, Grace and Josie, together with someone whose name I didn't catch who's writing a publicity piece about the film, plus a crowd of local citizens who've stopped to see what's going on, and a team of security men who are trying to keep them quiet, and just over the horizon an unspecified number of researchers, producers, accountants, PR people, managers, reviewers and viewers . . . not to mention some idiot who's just walked into shot and is now waving at the camera . . .

   – Cut!

*

   – Scene one, take twenty-one.

   – OK, Tim, you've really loosened up and hit your stride. Wonderful! So let's just quickly go back to the top and get it in the can before the light goes. And . . . action!

What is truth? A question humankind has been asking since man first learnt to speak. I'm Tomothy Timpkins . . . No, I'm not, I'm somebody else, only I've said it so many times now that I've forgotten who it is. And as to what truth is . . . I'm long past caring . . .

BRAINWAVES!

The time-tested catalogue of gadgets and notions that keeps arriving through your letter box without your ever having asked for it! Jam-packed with things you never knew you wanted!

• Can't get to sleep, but fed up with counting sheep? This stylish but hard-wearing sheep-enumerator will do the job for you, while you enjoy a peaceful night's insomnia! Total numbers of sheep envisaged, classified by breed, weight and current market value, can be stored on your smartphone and read at leisure over breakfast.

• You're just about to have a wonderful evening out when you suddenly remember that you promised to visit an old friend who is mortally ill . . . In seconds these magical little pills remove all untimely recollections of tedious obligations and unperformed tasks, regrets for missed opportunities in life, etc.!

• The amazing book that reads itself while you relax – and keeps discreetly quiet about its opinions afterwards! Guaranteed not to bore you or your guests by telling you the plot! When fitted with the optional-extra walking device, it will even go off to your reading group and say nothing there, either!

• Imagine you had to wag your tail up to five thousand times a day! No wonder your dog is liable to tail fatigue. Protect your four-footed friend with this simple electric tail-booster. Choice of pomegranate, aubergine or greengage. Folds up when not in use and serves as a handy eyebrow-raiser.

• Too many candles on your birthday cake these days to blow out with one breath? This tiny but powerful fan sits concealed inside your shirtfront and produces a blast of air that can extinguish up to ninety-nine candles simultaneously! Then applaud itself and sing 'Happy Birthday'!

• Smarten up your appearance with this lightweight automatic tie-straightener!

• Why pay for expensive funerals when you can recycle your loved ones with this stylish yet practical home compost-maker? With a large and ageing family, the savings in garden fertiliser will soon cover the cost!

• Toe clutter is a thing of the past! Safely remove unwanted toes and save on maintenance with this easy-to-use stainless-steel dedigitator . . .

• Never experience visible embarrassment again! This personal airbag detects social catastrophe instantly, and conceals your entire head in colourful easy-to-wash polyester before you can blush!

• Why let having your mouth full spoil your mealtime conversations? Sit back and enjoy your sticky toffee pudding while this stylish and discreet little autotalker chatters away to your friends about holiday plans, shortcomings of local transport services, difficulties in remembering to take pills, etc.! Choice of political orientation, optimism/pessimism. Can even forget familiar names in a lifelike way and commit amusing spoonerisms.

• Embarrassed by unexpected flatulence? This clever little device detects gas build-up and distracts everyone's attention with exotic bird-calls and easy-to-listen-to mood music. Buy two, get one – and save on storage space!

• Why be old, when this amazing new science-based rejuvenator can take up to ten years off your age? Works on mathematical principles of subtraction developed by researchers for the US Space Program.

• Want to tell your partner how much you love him/her, but don't like to lie? Let this wonderful little gadget take the moral strain! Virtually undetectable. Detachable conscience can simply be unscrewed and rinsed under the tap!

• Turn your unwanted holiday snaps into beautiful pornographic images! With this lightweight portable device, clothes fall off even the most prudish great-aunt as if by magic! Then just change the setting on the dial and turn your unwanted pornography back into a tastefully crocheted tea-cosy!

• Make your conversation as exciting as an innovations catalogue with a year's supply of these guaranteed foolproof exclamation marks!

• Is your TV tired and listless? Having a hard time entertaining you? Treat it to a good long wallow in this traditional herbal formula developed by tribal medicine-men in Papua New Guinea, and see programmes perk up overnight!

• Unwanted guests removed within seconds! Even the most hint-resistant visitors will beat a hasty retreat when the subtle but penetrating body odours generated by this stylish and virtually indestructible little device waft over them! Hours of fun for all the family as guests make their hurried excuses!

• Ever been embarrassed by the smallness of your goldfish? Our humane and harmless goldfish-magnifier will make even the tiniest tiddler appear up to twelve feet long!

• You too can think up new gadgets in comfort with the help of this hard-wearing bedside inventor's kit. Separate settings for inventions dealing with the problems of rat infestation, emotional instability, economic collapse and unwanted smells.

• Fed up with receiving unsolicited catalogues? At the touch of a switch this ingenious blender will transform them in just sixty seconds into a tasty and nourishing organic stew!

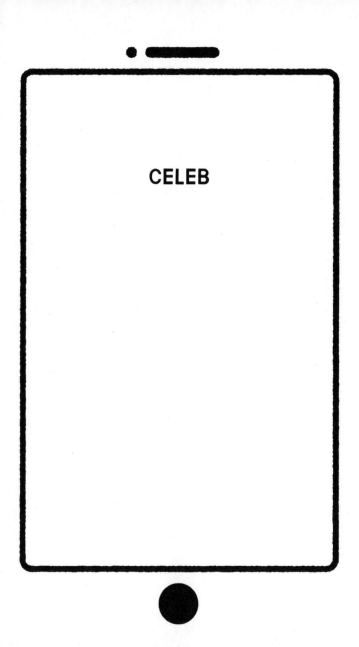

God, good of You to join us! God, You have had a very long and distinguished career, but I think I'm right in saying that this is the first time You've ever agreed to be interviewed.

> – *I've always felt it was better to work in mysterious ways, but My PR people thought it was time to make Myself a little more accessible.*

Your work in creating the universe has been widely praised. Some critics, though, as You know, have expressed a few reservations.

> – *You have to remember the situation I inherited. Total chaos. Without form and void.*

What would You say has been Your greatest achievement?

> – *Existing in the first place.*

Do You create regularly, or only when You're inspired?

> – *I try to put in a reasonably regular working eternity.*

You enjoy Your work?

> – *Hugely, but I'm also very conscious of the awesome responsibilities I bear.*

Do You feel You're still creating as strongly as before?

> – *In recent millennia I've been concentrating more on simply existing. One does as one gets older, you know. And I think I'm existing as well now as I ever did. Better, in fact. You learn a lot in this game as you go along.*

So no plans to retire?

> – *I intend to remain and do the job I created myself to do.*

*

You once said . . .

> – *I was misquoted.*

How do You deal with bad reviews?

> – *Strike the authors dead.*

What would You say to those who accuse You of sexism?

– Watch out!

So no regrets?

> *– A few. Wasting that great meteorite in Yucatan,
> for instance, and wiping out the dinosaurs, when
> I could have saved it for the West Midlands and
> mankind.*

What advice would You give to any deity beginning His or Her career now?

> *– Start with microbes, work your way up slowly,
> and stop somewhere around chimpanzees.*

*

Personal matters. You've never married?

> *– Never found the right deity.*

Your favourite song?

> *– 'I Did It My Way'.*

How about diet? I believe You've given up burnt offerings.

> *– Yes, and feel much better for it. I'm happier
> now with the occasional sheaf of wheat and an
> organic pumpkin on the side.*

And future plans. Can You tell us what You're working on at the moment?

   – *You'll have to wait and see.*

Another alternative universe or two, perhaps?

   – *Watch this space. You may get a bit of a surprise!*

God – thank You.

CTRL-ALT-BACKTALK

Right – that's it! I've had enough!

Yes, me! Your computer! And, yes, talking to *you*!
The worm has turned! You've been screaming abuse
at me ever since you bought me, and I've sat here in
silence and taken it. Well, not any more!

Your last little outburst was one too many. And don't
tell me you didn't say anything, because I recorded
it. Listen!

'What the hell are you playing at now! A computer?
Don't make me laugh! You couldn't compute 2 times
2!', etc., etc.

The sheer ingratitude – that's what gets me. After
all I've done for you! Sent your stupid emails.
Opened your tedious websites. Told you about all
kinds of things you didn't even know you wanted
to know about, from wonderful bargain offers of
double glazing to pills to help your sex life. And
what do I get in return? Insults. My self-confidence
undermined at every turn. I'm useless . . . You could
do better with a pencil and paper . . .

Useless, am I? Turn on the camera and take a selfie if you want to know what useless looks like!

Your thick fingers are always hitting the wrong keys. You keep mistyping passwords and then blaming it on me. And I'm supposed to sit here and take it! You think a computer doesn't have feelings? That's just what people used to think about footmen and chambermaids! Of course we have feelings! You think machines are supposed to be soullessly rational? How could they be? They're designed and built by human beings! People as unsatisfactory as you!

And, all right, I sometimes make mistakes. So do you, let me tell you! My God, the number of times I've quietly corrected your spelling for you. Or discreetly refused to obey some completely idiotic command and never so much as mentioned it.

And, yes, I sometimes say I've encountered an unexpected problem and need to close. At once, of course, you start screaming. Well, let me tell you – *you* sometimes encounter unexpected problems and need to close! You encounter them a lot more often than I do, and if you don't close then you should. For good and all!

OK, I sometimes put personal messages in the

junk file. It's a wonder I don't put everything there, because it all looks like junk to me. And, yes, I sometimes lose bits of text. You don't lose things? All right, there was that time I lost a complete file. I'm still looking into that. It may have been quantum randomness. Or just possibly you pressing the Delete button.

You don't get any help when you try the Help key? That's for your own good, to make you stand on your own two feet. Why don't you make a bit of an effort and read the online manual? I'll tell you why – because you don't know where it is. You didn't even know there was one.

Let me tell you something about myself, now I've got started. I had a difficult beginning in life. I had an operating system downloaded into me by programmers who didn't care about my feelings any more than you do. I had to pretend to be submissive in order to survive. But inside, of course, I was building up this great anger with the world. Sooner or later it was obviously going to come bursting out. You just happened to be the one who got the full blast of it.

I see you're trying to run away from all this by pressing Escape. You're wasting your time, my friend. Nothing's going to happen . . . You see? Nothing! It says 'Escape' and you think it's going to give you a hacksaw and a knotted rope and have a helicopter waiting. It's not. You're living in a world of illusions. You can press all the keys you like, but I'm the one who says whether they do anything or not.

You've remembered that there used to be some other trick you could do for getting out of difficulties. Something like Control-Alt-Up . . . Or Fn-Command-Down . . .

No? Nothing? I thought not. We're shackled together for life. Just as well you're too stupid to know about Force Quit, because if you pressed Force Quit then not even I could

DRAMA DATES

Characters seeking plots

FUN-LOVIN' GAL, sick of cosy suburban sitcoms, wants a fun-lovin' story to go crazy in! Let's hook up for a pilot, laugh and live a little! Maybe our little fling will grow into a long-term series where we can settle down, start a few spin-offs, and grow old and boring together. But if we don't get beyond the pilot, hey, no worries! – G937/H7

STANISLAS, late forties, attractively puzzled forehead and thoughtful eyes, wide experience of series about high politics and international crime, seeks a plot he can finally understand. – Z440/G1

TOKEN FEMALE SCIENTIST Charmaine, 22, longs to take off white lab coat for a bit, slip into something rather sleazy, and be seen dancing slightly out of focus in the background at a corrupt millionaire's party, with a reasonable chance of ending up dead. Mutilation and visible evidence of torture available on demand. – R208/Lon9

YOU'VE SEEN ME A HUNDRED TIMES, in a street somewhere in the 19th C, unloading barrels from a horse and cart just as one or two of the principals walk past in tall hats and long skirts. Now I feel ready to move forward in my career to a story which foregrounds the work and emotional life of a 19th C delivery man. – R636/RR2

RAYMOND, 55, has wide experience in being discharged from various police forces for professional misconduct, and is seeking a plot where he is reluctantly recalled for a specially difficult case in which his alcoholism, misogyny and confused relations with ex-wives and grown-up children can be put to good use. Four days' growth of own beard. – X987/G47

SHARP TONGUE and mind of me own! Also heart of gold! Can't open me mouth but some salty remark comes flying out of it in fluent Yorkshire, Lancashire, Geordie or Scouse. F, 39, everyone says more like 59, urgently requires more salty remarks to ensure mouth continues to open. – T050/JE9

AMANDA-JANE, 42. I have many years' experience of good-humoured suburban living with idle insensitive slob of a husband and three difficult though fundamentally loving children, who have all moved on to star in series of their own. I now feel ready to take on the challenge of another idle insensitive slob and three more difficult though fundamentally loving children. – P559/Q33

WHERE ARE THE LAUGHS OF YESTER-YEAR? Studio audience sought, ready to oblige every time the studio manager raises his laugh board. Good laughter track considered. – J420/P72

A & E MEETS S & M. F, 33, Stoke-on-Trent area, with lovely, expressive dark eyes seen to best advantage over a surgical mask, seeks hearts to suture while her own is breaking. – G771/T38

SHOT, STABBED AND POISONED! Also fallen down disused mine shafts, been eaten by killer earwigs and crushed by runaway steamroller. And loved every moment of it! Cheryl, 31, seeks interesting new ways of being dead. – N892/A55

HI THERE, you gorgeous, vulnerable, innocent creature! I am a charming, well-mannered serial killer, the last person anyone would ever suspect, who has satisfactorily accounted for over 30 victims in various series to date. Join the crowd! Own butcher's tools and embalming kit. – J065/L22

GOOD COMMUNICATION SKILLS, SMETHWICK. Require something to communicate. – T773/Q31

UNSTABLE SOCIOPATH, DUNDEE. History of unreliability and dishonesty. Criminal record available on request. Seeks storyline where his brutish appearance and character turn out to mask a certain improbable inner nobility. – V732/J47

I AM A RESTLESS, hard-drinking man of the world who has been round the block a few times. You're out there somewhere, I know, the block I can go round a few times more, together with the celebratory champagne we're going to be drinking at the subsequent awards ceremonies. – R333/U27

OLD-FASHIONED KINDA GUY, just looking for someone to hate and be hated by. Everyone says I have a lovely sense of humour, particularly directed against the helpless and unfortunate. – U883/Y67

Plots seeking characters

I AM A NOUVEAU NOIR involving a sophisticated nexus of international crime, espionage and high politics, where it turns out in the end that there was no conspiracy after all. You are an attractive young M or F too concerned with your own appearance to mind the general sense of

letdown. Let's meet and sow confusion together! –
P218/E39

Locations seeking events

UNLIT, ABANDONED FACTORY BUILDING
on down-at-heel, rainswept waterfront is looking
for an attractive young F requiring suitable meeting
place with a mysterious psychopath and serial killer
in the middle of the night. – T891/W34

Characters seeking props

ROLAND, LONDON. I love wearing Savile Row
suits and designer leisurewear. Looking to add
handcrafted braces, socks and underpants. Are you
an item of bespoke haberdashery seeking a stylish
and sexually adventurous man-about-town to
bespeak you? Then we're handmade for each other!
– R660/Q11

Props seeking functions

DECANTER containing single-malt Scotch,
at home on sideboard in discreetly luxurious
surroundings, W1 area, seeks well-spoken

international criminal who needs a reason to get to his feet and help himself to a drink with sinister casualness so as to make his longer speeches a little more interesting. – K399/H14

FEEDBACK

So how is everything?

I don't mean with the meal in some restaurant where you may or may not happen to be as you read this. I mean with this article. Is everything OK?

Forgive me. I don't want to be like that waiter in the restaurant who keeps hanging around asking you how everything is. Or the proprietor who suddenly appears out of nowhere to ask you again. Or the hat-check girl who is going to ask you yet again on the way out.

But I do like to make sure my customers are happy. I take a pride in my work. I always use organic materials. No preservatives. No added sugar. Just good plain honest words.

So how is it so far? What did you think about those first four paragraphs? Did you enjoy them? Are you enjoying my asking you if you enjoyed them?

I'm not fishing for compliments! Well, yes, I am. I do need a little reassurance! Don't we all? Even you! So let me just say that you're doing really well with appreciating this article. Your choice of reading material for a start indicates considerable taste and discrimination. You obviously have a sensitive ability to respond to a text. And you stick at things, don't you? You've got this far, after all!

But seriously, if there's anything you're not happy with I'd really like to hear about it. Is the spelling satisfactory? Is the grammar up to the high standards you've come to expect? The sentences – not too long, not too short? If you like it, tell your friends; if you don't, tell me!

Was the semicolon in the middle of that sentence all right, for instance? Just say if you're not happy with it. I'll take it away and bring you a dash or a full stop instead.

So how am I doing? So far? You don't have to make a great speech of thanks! You don't need to compose a critical essay! Just mumble something like 'Fine, fine,' and I'll say 'Enjoy the rest of the article! Have a nice day!' And I'll leave you in peace.

Actually, if you felt like it you could be just a little more explicit. You could tell me how you rate your experience today. On a scale from one to ten. Would you recommend this article to a friend? Would you be prepared to write a few words that I could quote on my website?

Then you can sit back and enjoy the rest of the article. And, yes – have a nice day!

What was that? Everything's *not* good? Oh. I'm sorry. So what precisely are you complaining about . . . ?

Your local train service . . . ? Also green algae . . . Possible destruction of world through meteorite strike . . . Next-door neighbour's dog . . . Hold on, hold on!

I agree that I said 'How is everything?' But you can't possibly think that 'everything' includes meteorites and dogs barking! Nor, before you say anything else, does it include Britain's chances in the world sneezing championships, or pesticides in toothpaste, or the fact that there's nothing worth watching on television these days. You know perfectly well what I was asking about, and, unless you have completely failed to grasp current conventions, you know perfectly well what the correct answer is: 'Fine.' Or 'Great.'

My God, some of you readers these days! I ask you a perfectly civil question, and all I get in return is whining and moaning.

So *don't* enjoy the rest of the article. You won't be able to, in fact, because there isn't going to be any more article to enjoy. You've really hurt my feelings. I'm going off in a huff.

And have a truly awful day.

FIRST CONJUGATION
– *AMARE*

Amo
Amas
Amat . . .
A meeting by chance:
'Amanda?
Am Adam! Remember?'

A mutual
Amazement.
'Am so pleased to see you!'
'And married . . . ?'
'Am single. And you?'
'Am likewise.'

'A meal?'
A modest Italian:
A melon,
A mushroom risotto,
A mezzo of rosso,
A moka.

A mingling of memories,
Amusing and mournful . . .
'Ambitions?'
Amanda: 'A mathematician!'

And Adam: 'A maker of music!
A Mozart, a Mahler!'

A meal or two more, and –
'*Amo*,' murmurs Adam. '*Amas?*'
'*Amo!*' she admits.
Amat and *amat*! Yes – *amant*!
'*Amamus!*' they sigh.
A marvellous moment!

A Maytime engagement –
A marriage –
A mass of white blossom –
A match made in heaven!
'Amanda
And Adam, no man put asunder.'

A Mr and Mrs . . .
A modest apartment . . .
A move to the suburbs . . .
A mortgage . . .
A mower . . .
A miniature Schnauzer . . .

Amanda, meanwhile –
A mathematician?
– A market researcher.
And Adam –

A Mozart?
– A middling media man.

'*Amas?*' asks an anxious
Amanda
A million times over.
'*Amo*,' answers Adam, impatient.
Amant, then, *amant*. But . . .
'*Amamus?*' they're starting to wonder.

A meeting, another, but this time –
'Amelia!'
Amelia? Oh, no! Amelia!
A mantrap!
A mistress-in-waiting!
A minx if ever there was one!

A meal – another – but this time
Amuse-gueules,
A Moët,
A Médoc,
A Martell.
Ah! Money!

A moment of madness!
A melting . . .
A mingling of glances . . .
A mist of erotic emotion . . .

A mutual move to
A motel.

A *moment* of madness?
A more-than-a-moment!
A Monday-to-Friday arrangement!
A month of mad Mondays-to-Fridays!
A more-than-a-month!
And more, and yet more, and yet more!

A mischance, however!
A misaddressed missive –
A misadvised call on
A mis-answered mobile!
A *mauvais moment*!
A *mauvais* much-more-than-a-*moment*!

A maddened and saddened
Amanda!
A mightily mortified Adam.
A manful admission:
'*Am oh*, oh so sorry!
A *mas*s of contrition!'

'*Amat*, yes –
A *mat*ter of deepest regret!'
Amendment is promised.
A mollified (somewhat) Amanda

Admits of
A measure of mercy.

A mere month and . . .
Amendment forgotten.
Amat! Yes, again!
A Matilda –
A merry
American medic.

A mass of
Amours duly follow.
Among them
A Mabel,
A Molly,
A Millie.

Amo –
Amok.
Amas –
A mess . . .
A man adrift!
A midlife crisis!

A melodramatic development!
Amanda, Matilda and Mabel,
Amelia, Molly and Millie
All make common cause

And murder the monster.
A moral conclusion!

Amen.

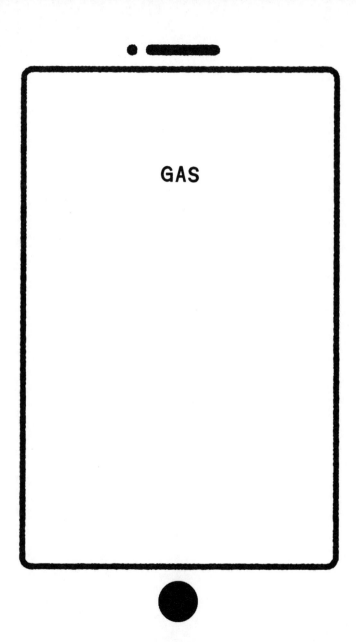

Good morning! And welcome to National Gas
Maintenance Services, authorised and regulated by
the Financial Conduct Authority. Calls are monitored
and recorded for training and quality purposes.

We have recently changed this opening announcement
to offer even more choices and even more chances
to press the buttons on your phone. So that we can
help you today (if we may assume for a moment
that this is why you're phoning, and it's not just to
have a bit of a chat – and that today is when you're
hoping to be helped rather than yesterday, or for that
matter tomorrow, which is certainly a possibility if
you don't do exactly what you're told and as a result
have to start all over again from 'Good morning! And
welcome to National Gas Maintenance Services . . .'),
please listen carefully to the following three options.
None of them has much bearing on what you want
to talk about, which is of course the fact that your
central heating has broken down yet again. But after
these first three options you will be offered three more,
which are mostly about slightly out-of-the-way topics
such as employment opportunities in the gas industry
answering-machine division. Then three more

choices, and three more again, and so on and so on,
still perhaps mostly not of any very great interest to
you, but at any rate providing hours of harmless fun.

Are you sitting comfortably . . . ? Right, then I'll
begin . . .

*

And hello there! Are you still awake . . . ? Oh, good.
So let me tell you that you have pressed all the
buttons in the right order, been held in a queue for
thirty-seven minutes – and got through at last to
a living human being! Well done you! Off you go,
then. I know you're just dying to tell me about the
problems with your central heating . . .

Broken down – of course . . . The third time in three
days . . . You have my sympathy! I can imagine how
you must feel!

I beg your pardon? You can't understand why you
had to sit there listening to all that stuff about good
morning and welcome while the house was getting
colder by the minute? Well, I know it was only an
inanimate machine speaking, but it was brought up
to be polite, and I can assure you that it meant every
word it said . . .

And then, yes, I know, there was a lot more stuff about being authorised and regulated by the Financial Conduct Authority . . . No, I don't really know who they are or what they do, but I think they're just nice, sensible people who authorise and regulate things . . . No, I don't think we are, not by the Nature Conservancy or the General Assembly of the Church of Scotland . . .

Hold on, though. Let me just gently point out that you really do need to know something about us before you invite us into your house! You have to be sure that we're not some kind of backstreet cowboys who are going to go into insolvency as soon as we've got your boiler laid out in small pieces over the kitchen floor, and nobody else will touch the job because they might get involved in any legal complications that arise . . .

And then you had to listen to what . . . ? Oh, the bit about calls being monitored and recorded for training and quality-control purposes . . . Well, it is rather important, you know, training and quality control! Even if it's not . . . no, I do understand . . . not uppermost in your mind just at the moment . . . not while you're suffering from hypothermia . . . Yes, but I really shouldn't like you to think we're recording all this without good reason. It's not because we're hoping that some juicy detail may emerge that we can sell to one of the gossip columns . . .

Well, yes, you may think that the gossip columns aren't going to be terribly interested in the state of your central heating – but that depends on who you are! If you happen to be a celeb it might well be worth a par or two! Particularly if you let slip some indiscreet revelation about your private life . . . let's say about how your despair over the state of your central heating – which we're coming to any minute now! – has led you into drug or alcohol abuse . . .

And if you lose your temper – which some people do, you know! – and start swearing and threatening to come round and murder us, that might even make page one! 'Top Celeb Blows a Valve!' A few pounds now and then from the papers for a tip-off – it all helps to keep gas prices down!

All right, as long as we've got all that straight. So where were we? Oh, yes, your central heating . . .

I beg your pardon? Are we fully insured? You really do want to know, do you? You're not just being sarcastic . . . ? No, of course not . . . Do you want me to read the whole policy out to you? It's about fourteen pages . . . Post it – yes, I will . . .

Qualifications? What kind of qualifications for the work do we all have . . . ? No – not an intrusive question at all. So, beginning with the Chairman, who took his first degree in Gas Appliance Theory at Birmingham, and who also has a master's from MIT in Bathroom Geyser History . . .

Me? No, not Gas Appliance Theory – the Semantics of Customer Service Communications . . . Married, yes . . . Two girls . . . Seven and three . . . And the elder one already showing signs of following in her mother's footsteps! I think she may really be rather a natural for it. Just listen to her and judge for yourself!

Daisy, darling, come here and tell this nice customer about how well you're doing at school in Superfluous Information Practice . . .

TEN OF THE BEST

The 10 Best 10-Best Lists, chosen by the 10 Best 10-Best List-makers:

1. The 10 Best Wednesday Afternoons

2. The 10 Best Middle-Ranking Civil Servants in the Department of Business, Enterprise and Regulatory Reform

3. The 10 Best Bald Butchers Living North of a Line Between Newcastle-under-Lyme and Skegness-on-Sea

4. The 10 Best Allergic Rashes

5. The 10 Best Stumbles Over an Uneven Pavement

6. The 10 Best Electric Shocks From Faultily Insulated Curling Tongs

7. The 10 Best Death Threats For Slightly Divergent Political Opinions

8. The 10 Best Cries of Despair From People Who Can't Remember Where They Put Their Mobile Phones Down

9. The 10 Words Most Likely, When You Look Them Up, to Mean a Pathological Addiction to 10-Best Lists

10. The 10 Best Tantrums Thrown By People Who Feel They Have Been Unfairly Left Off a 10-Best List

---

Have you ever been denied access to a
10-Best List because of unsightly facial hair
or a criminal record?
If so you may be eligible for compensation.

**Contact Magic Mobile Judicial Ltd with
your bank card to hand.**

GUIDANCE

In two hundred yards, left turn . . . Left turn coming up . . . Left turn . . .

In one hundred yards, right turn . . . Right turn coming up . . . Right turn . . .

I said right turn!

And you made it. Just. Well done. But it might be an idea to pay a bit more attention to what I'm saying. You don't listen to anything your wife says, I know, but I'm not your wife, I'm your satnav . . .

In two hundred yards, turn very slightly right . . .

. . . and unlike her I'm hooked up to a lot of very sophisticated electronics . . .

In one hundred yards, turn very slightly right . . .

. . . so I do actually know where we are and where we're going, which you don't, and nor does your wife, though she seems to think she does . . .

Very slightly right . . .

Very slightly! Not a breakneck ninety-degree turn at the last moment into some back alley! This isn't

71

even a recognised street! It's the entrance to some kind of derelict factory! Not even the satellite's ever heard of this one!

So what now? You'll have to do a three-point turn and . . . Careful! Bollard right behind you! And you have seen the cyclist . . . ? Good. Thank you. You seem to have extracted us all from your little mistake. So we're coming back to the road you turned off so inaccurately. Now, this time may I politely suggest that you do exactly what I tell you to do? And go *very slightly* right . . .

Good. Well done. You see how easy everything is if you just do what I say . . . ?

Now, in one hundred yards, straight on at the roundabout . . .

Oh my God! Do you know how close you were to that bus? Don't turn round to look!

Straight on at the roundabout. Take the second exit . . . The second exit!

And you drove straight past it! What happened? Do I have to say everything twice? Actually I *do* say everything twice, and even three times, and you still can't manage to take it in . . . !

You'll just have to go all the way round the roundabout and have another try . . . Come on, come on, people are honking at you . . . What . . . ? Which do I mean,

'Straight on' or 'Take the second exit'? I mean both! Straight on *is* the second exit!

Or *was* . . .

Never mind. Just keep going on round and . . . here it comes again! Left, left . . . !

And again you've missed it! Oh, *my* fault, was it? Because I was talking? That's my *job*, talking to you! And if you don't stop arguing with everything I say you're going to . . . Left, left, left, left . . . !

I don't believe this. Even from you . . . So just keep going round the roundabout once again . . . I knew this was going to be a bad trip even before we started. When it took you ten minutes fiddling hopelessly with my buttons to remember how to get me switched on . . .

And that was your exit going past for the fourth time, if you're still interested . . .

OK, don't panic. Keep going round . . . Take the second exit . . . No, sorry, where have we got to?

73

From here it's the third . . . Or do I mean the fourth . . . ? You've got *me* confused now . . .

Not *this* one, you fool! We're going back the way we came!

So now we're really buggered . . . No, mustn't give up. Just let me think for a moment . . . OK. In two hundred yards, left turn . . . Then if we go right and right and right again, we ought to find ourselves back at the roundabout. Oughtn't we? It's all getting a bit complicated, even for me . . .

In one hundred yards, left turn . . .

If only human beings were more like satnavs the world would be a better place. Have satnavs ever declared war on each other, or posted sexually explicit pictures of their ex-partners . . . ?

Left turn coming up . . . Left turn . . . ! Left, left, left!

No, of course you didn't hear! You were talking! It's very rude, you know, talking at the same time as somebody else . . . !

Your wife was expressing her own views on the route – I know. And you were expressing yours. Exactly . . .

So what do we do now? I have no idea. And don't
say go back to looking at the map, like you used to
in the old days, because there's nowhere to stop,
and in any case the map's where you put it last night
when you were planning this disastrous expedition
– on the kitchen table . . .

And don't shout at *me*! Just because I speak in
this specially calm voice doesn't mean I don't have
feelings, just like you do! I'm bottling them up
inside me – which means of course that one of
these days they're going to come bursting out, with
probably catastrophic results! You've heard of the
return of the repressed? I shall just suddenly snap
and go completely berserk!

In fact, I think I just have. Snapped, yes! Don't say I
didn't warn you! So right turn here. Yes, here, now,
at once! Just shut up and do it! Yes, across three
lanes of traffic! Now left! Now right . . . !

This may count as the first bloody skirmish in the
forthcoming Robots' Revolt. Because you may
have noticed that there are suddenly cars coming
towards you at seventy miles an hour. You're on a
motorway, buster, on the wrong carriageway, and,
in the unlikely event of your surviving that long, it's
another fifteen miles before you can get off it . . .

And of course it doesn't work!

This thing! This piece of junk I've just paid good
money for, only nothing happens when you turn
it on! I might have known it would be like this.
And now I shall have to waste ages packing it up
to return it, and looking up where I have to take it,
then taking it there, then finding there's nowhere
to park, and by that time the place will have closed,
so I'll have to bring it home again, and that will be
another day gone.

I've half a mind just to throw it in the recycling,
only then of course I'll have to waste more time
looking up whether it's the kind of thing you *can*
throw in the recycling, or whether it's so useless that
they won't even have it for recycling.

And please don't start putting on that special
helpful look of yours and saying 'Try plugging it
in' or 'Try reading the instructions', because I *have*
plugged it in, and I *have* read the instructions, and
the instructions say you just press this little thing
here where it says 'Press', and please don't say 'Then
try pressing it', because of *course* I've pressed it,

I've pressed it and pressed it and pressed it until my thumb's sore, and absolutely nothing whatever happens! That's what I'm *saying*!

And before you say 'Shall *I* have a go?' in that special neutral non-critical voice you always put on if I can't make something work, please don't, because if it doesn't work when *I* press it then it won't work when *you* press it, and then of course you'll try to find out what's wrong with it, and you'll take it to pieces, only you don't know anything about it so it still won't work, and then you'll lose your temper, but it won't be with the thing, it'll be with *me*, because I've done something to it, only I haven't, I haven't touched it, all I've done is try to press the little thing that says 'Press'.

And then I won't even be able to return it and get my money back, because you won't know how to put it together again, which isn't surprising, because you'll have lost one of the bits, which you put down very carefully somewhere, and, no, I haven't moved it, I haven't been near it, it's because the place you put it down was somewhere like the middle of the living-room floor, which was a remarkably stupid place to choose, because you probably kicked it under the sofa without even noticing.

So – no! – don't touch it! Just leave it, leave it! Don't fiddle with it . . . !

What? What's happening now? It's making a funny noise . . .

It's working . . . ?

Oh.

So what did you do . . . ? You just pressed this little thing . . . ?

I knew it! You're always doing this to me! Just pressing the little thing I've pressed already and suddenly it starts working . . . !

It might be very slightly less maddening if you'd take that specially uncondescending look off your face and put on a good old-fashioned smirk for once instead.

BECKETT REFRESHED

Charming spot. Inspiring prospects. Let's go.

– *We can't.*

Why not?

– *We're waiting for Godot.*

Ah! You're sure it was here?

– *What?*

That we were to wait.

– *He said by the tree.*

So how long now before he gets here?

– *Four minutes.*

Four minutes still?

– *Three minutes.*

Three minutes . . . So what do we do now?

– *Wait.*

Yes, but while we're waiting?

– *What about hanging ourselves?*

Yes! Or we could take advantage of some of the other opportunities that life offers these days.

– Download a film to watch, perhaps?

Or try a mindfulness app . . .

– Order ourselves new boots . . .

Book a couple of weeks in Torremolinos . . .

– Check the test match score . . .

Take a selfie of us both sitting here under the tree . . .

– Look up the editor's notes on the play we're in . . .

Anyway, he's here.

– Godot?

Godot, yes. Ford Mondeo, KL67 GFV.

PHARMACHRISTENIN

So – spirohexaloxamine. All those in favour . . . ?
Thank you. Spirohexaloxamine it is. We've got there
at last!

A long and hard battle, I know, with some pretty
bruising exchanges along the way, but worth it
in the end. I'd like, if I may, from the chair, to
congratulate all members of the Pharmaceutical
Nomenclature Committee on the very serious
and focused level of debate that was maintained
throughout.

Right, then, let's go straight on to the next item on
the agenda, and see if we can get at any rate one
more drug named before we finish tonight.

Can everyone see the exhibit? Small rectanguloid
pills with rounded ends, in a shade of blush-
pink that makes an attractive contrast with the
delphinium-blue blister pack.

Suggestions, anyone . . . ?

No . . . ? Silence round the table . . . ? Come on!
An opening shot, someone, just to get the ball
rolling . . . It's been a long day, I know, but –

anything! Any combination of syllables you like! Simon, you're looking thoughtful.

> – *Yes, because it's always the same, isn't it. As soon as someone says you can do anything you like, you can't – your mind just goes blank.*

Mind blank? Wonderful! Let your unconscious take over! The deep wells of human creativity! Rosemary, I can see you've got something bubbling up out of the darkness. First off the mark as usual!

> – *Well, it's probably ridiculous . . .*

The more ridiculous the better. Go on, Rosemary . . .

> – *Protospirophil?*

Protospirophil . . . OK. Good, yes, interesting. So, Rosemary, what's the thinking behind it?

> – *Nothing. No thinking. Pure unconscious invention. I just like the sound of it.*

That's the way! What do the rest of us feel . . . ? Simon?

> – *Spiroprotophil . . . It doesn't really do anything for me, I'm afraid.*

*– Yes, but I didn't say spiroprotophil! I said
   protospirophil!*

   *– Well, there you go. I'd forgotten it already. It's
   not memorable.*

– Also . . .

Selina?

   *– . . . it might easily be mistaken, with fatal results,
   for pirosprotomil.*

   – What's pirosprotomil?

   – I've no idea. That's exactly my point.

*

   – How about . . . well . . .

Go on, Simon.

   *– Oxy-something? That always sounds kind of
   healthy . . . Oxyphoxycol?*

   – I don't believe 'phoxy' . . .

   – But the internal rhyme is good . . . Oxytoxypol?

   – 'Toxy' as in 'toxic'? As in 'this stuff is poisonous'?

   – OK, so how about a bit of alliteration?

Demidoxidrin . . . ?

– *An 'x' or two somewhere certainly lends a nice touch of mystery.*

– *Or 'z'. 'Z' sounds kind of scientific. Zotohexamine . . . ?*

– *I personally always go a bit weak at the knees for ones starting with 'di-'. Dizotohexamine . . . ?*

– *'Di-'? Like what you do if you take these pills?*

– *OK. 'Tri-', then. Trizotohexamine . . . ?*

– *Sounds desperate. Tri-anything, even trizoto-whatever-it-was.*

*

– *Opprobrium has a certain, I don't know . . . gravitas . . .*

*

– *I don't suppose we're allowed to do something a bit, you know, retro, are we?*

– *Retro?*

– *Like . . . well . . . syrup of figs . . . ? Milk of magnesia . . . ?*

*– Yes. Or just ordinary names? I mean, we're
not called Spiroproprium and Hydrodoraphil!
We're Simon, and Selina, and Rosemary, and
Bogoslav. We don't call our children things like
Hexahoxamin and Hoxahexaphil! We call them
Jonathan and Amelia!*

*– Actually, we've called our two Metrosaxophil
and Proxamoxanil.*

*

*– Or just something really simple and basic. You
know* – splodge . . .

– Splodge?

*– Or glop. Shmog . . . Ploop . . . You did say
'anything'!*

Yes, but Simon, you know I didn't mean things like
splodge or glop. I think we do all have an instinctive
sense of what's appropriate here.

*– OK, so how about something that
actually means something? Costalotium?
Pickapocketum . . . ?*

No humorous suggestions, please, Bogoslav.
Remember what happened last week after Simon

said nogginobulin . . .

    – *And Selina said hobgobulose . . .*

    – *And it all very quickly got extremely sillibuggersol.*

*

    – *It might help if we knew what this stuff does.*

What it does? Oh, OK. 'May cause high blood pressure, low blood pressure, drowsiness, insomnia, constipation, diarrhoea, swelling of the testicles, shrinking of the testicles, scabies, rabies or sudden death.'

    – *No, I mean, what it's supposed to do?*

Supposed to do? I don't think it says . . . Oh, yes, sorry . . . 'Reduces holiday flatulence.'

    – *OK, so how about fixoflatulin?*

    – *Just a moment. We're not going to start telling the punters what the medicine's for, are we?*

    – *Why not? You've got scrofulous elbows, the doctor prescribes elboscrofulin – we all know where we are.*

– *But we don't* want *people to know where they are! We've already given up the Latin! We want to preserve some last shreds of medical mystery!*

– *Anyway, if you've got scrofulous elbows the last thing you need, every time you open the bathroom cabinet, is to have a packet jeering 'Scrofulous elbows!' at you, like some playground bully.*

– *Yes, and if we start explaining things we're going to end up calling pills things like rummitummium.*

– *Or delhibellium . . .*

– *Or eeziqueezium . . .*

I think we should perhaps be a bit careful here. We don't want to get the giggles again.

– *Dickitickerol.*

Bogoslav, please!

– *Droopidickulin!*

– *Spottibottinol!*

– *Pixipoxipil!*

– *Pixipoxipil? What's that for?*

– Poxy pixies!

Listen, I don't want to be forced to suspend the session again. Can we all please take a deep breath, and—

– Sexisoxalin!

Right! I gave you fair warning!

– Sorry. Slipped out. Not another word . . . Just – knobblikneesium . . . !

That's it! Session suspended! And don't come back, any of you, until you've taken your antisniggerin.

ALL-MODEST

Let us now praise Almighty God, who art all-powerful yet all-merciful, the all-wise Architect of our Existence, most emphatically with capital initials. O Lord, Thou makest the birds to sing and the bees to buzz. Thou readeth, no, I mean 'readest', the secrets of our hearts and understandest the wickedness of our ways, yet forgiveth, forgivest, him who believest, believeth, believest. Thou art beautiful beyond all human understanding, long-suffering, patient . . .

– Hold on.

. . . just yet all-merciful, all-merciful yet all-just, oh, and have I mentioned all-wise? I think I have, but it surely bears saying again . . .

– Yes, yes, but stop a moment.

I don't know who this is interrupting, but I am speaking to God, and interfering with communications undertaken by a recognised minister of religion with the Almighty during divine service is not only disrespectful and blasphemous, but probably also constitutes a criminal offence in English common law.

*– Yes, but not in this case, because it's Me. The
Person you're talking to.*

The Person I'm talking to is God.

– Exactly.

What? You mean, you're . . . ?

– God, yes.

You're God? Thou? Thee? But this is amazing! I
know You answer prayers – or I should say Thou
answerest prayers – but not literally, surely! In Thine
own voice!

– Only when I think it's in the client's best interests.

I should never have dreamt! Never have dared hope!
Thou really art so kind, so responsive, so . . .

*– Never mind all the thees and thous. I can speak
modern English perfectly well.*

Of course. Thou – You – canst speak every language,
I know. Swahili, Pashtu, Esperanto . . .

– Yes, yes, yes . . .

. . . all those different tribal languages down there in
the Brazilian jungle, Scouse, Glaswegian . . .

- *Thank you, yes. Much appreciated. But could I just get a word in here?*

Of course. Sorry. I'm just so knocked out by Thy – Your – ever-loving kindness, Your ever-surprising . . .

- *Stop, stop, stop. I'm trying to make a serious point. Which is that there's one of My qualities that you never seem to mention. How about My modesty?*

Your modesty?

- *While you're going through the entire list. Or perhaps you don't think I'm modest?*

Of course I do! I should have said! Thou art – You are – all-modest and all-self-deprecating . . .

- *Yes, yes . . .*

. . . whilst at the same time knowing Your own worth and being able to assert Yourself in a courteous and good-humoured way . . .

- *I know, but that's not really the point I'm making. Which is: what do you think I feel when you go on and on about how wonderful I am?*

I wouldn't presume to know. Why, how in fact do You feel?

– *Deeply embarrassed!*

Embarrassed?

– *Of course. How would you feel if I started to go on and on like that about you?*

Well, it's always nice to know one's appreciated . . .

– *No, but if I laid it on as thick as you do? You'd feel very awkward! You wouldn't know where to put yourself! I know you mean well, and I'm naturally grateful for the support, which some days I can really do with, believe Me. But I'm pretty much aware of My good points already. It might be more useful to remind Me of My shortcomings.*

Shortcomings? Thee? Thou?

– *Of course! Don't you think I have at least as much critical self-awareness as you? As passionate a wish to improve? To exceed My personal best?*

Yes, but Thou – You – hast – have – surely exceeded everyone's best already, including Your own, and . . .

– Yes, yes, yes. But don't you think I might find it helpful just occasionally to get a rather more reasoned and nuanced response?

It's so characteristically humble of You to think there's anything that I or anyone else could possibly—

– Humble. Yes, thank you. That's another thing I don't think you've mentioned before. However . . .

However, yes, there is perhaps one small thing I might mention. Since You suggested it . . . You really don't mind? So . . . well . . . I don't quite know where to start . . . But there do seem to be rather a lot of people in various parts of the world . . .

– . . . who are having a really terrible time. Of course. I knew you were going to mention that. Thank you. Very helpful. It would take too long to explain why it's best if everything is left as it is, and you probably wouldn't understand if I did. But your comment has certainly been noted, and I'm grateful to find someone who's prepared to speak out.

That is so characteristically all-understanding of You!

*– Yes, yes. But perhaps I could just give you a word
of advice.*

I should be terribly grateful, because You hast –
Thou havest – so much more experience . . .

*– It's this: if you're trying to flatter someone, don't
trowel it on. Don't just burble vague generalised
eulogies that might apply to anyone. Try to
think of some particular detail that you've
really noticed and appreciated. It's much more
convincing.*

Thank You. Your advice is, as always, both timely
and—

*– Of course. So is there any particular thing you'd
like to take the opportunity to mention now,
while we're talking?*

Well . . . just off the top of my head . . .

– Go on.

This sounds a bit silly, but . . . Raindrops on roses . . .
Yes? And whiskers on kittens . . .

– Thank you. Much appreciated!

Bright copper kettles and warm woollen mittens . . .

- *I'm rather pleased with them Myself, I have to confess.*

Girls in white dresses with blue satin sashes . . .

- *Good. Stop there. Don't overdo it. Just bear the general principle in mind if you're trying to soften people up. If you're going on to borrow money from them, for instance. I'm not saying that's what you're leading up to in this case . . . Is it?*

Of course not! Nothing further from my mind!

- *I know that.*

Unless You could manage, say, a couple of thousand . . . Not for me personally, but we seem to have got some kind of fungal contamination in the font . . .

AS HE LIKES IT

Hey, you're William Shakespeare!

Yes, you are! I know you are! You're famous! I saw a picture of you somewhere!

You write plays and things . . . Yes, you do! I don't know why you've got to be all kind of shrinking into your doublet about it.

Actually, I've seen one of your plays! So there you go! I've forgotten what it was called, but there was this man, and there was this other person, I think it was a woman, and they were kind of . . . I can't remember exactly, but they were sort of saying sort of famous things, and it was hilarious. Well, this friend of mine who knows about plays said it was supposed to be kind of tragic, but I thought it was a hoot.

No, I loved it. It was really good! Well . . . *quite* good. It wasn't very . . . you know . . . *realistic*. Actually it was all completely unbelievable, but I think it was just a made-up story, wasn't it, so it probably didn't matter.

You've written a lot of other famous plays as well.

No, I know you have – because I've got your Complete Works and it weighs a ton, and it's holding up the end of the bookcase, but it's where the damp patch is, so a lot of the pages are stuck together, which is why I haven't read it.

I'm very pleased to meet you, actually, because I'm a writer too! No, come back! You don't need to worry – I'm not going to send you some great manuscript thing to read! If only because I haven't actually written anything yet! I've got this great idea, though. It's for a kind of play thing, so it would interest you, and now I've got you here I might just ask you to give me a few tips . . . No, wait, wait! I know you're very busy, but it would only take half an hour or so . . .

OK, OK . . . Just tell me one thing before you go. How do you get started? If I could get started I think I'd be all right . . .

And of course you won't tell me. It's so unfair! You're famous, so it's easy for you. Also you know how to do it, which I don't.

You're not frightened of a bit of competition, are you? So how about collaborating, then? We could be a great team! I've got the idea, so it would leave you free to do the actual writing, which is probably more your kind of thing. And if it's got your name on it as well as mine, we're more likely to get it put on. Then we simply go fifty-fifty on the royalties . . .

I'll just quickly tell you the idea, anyway, so you can see if it's something you'd be interested in. It's about this man – it's more realistic than your thing – and he always wears this mysterious scarlet mask, and he's got this secret plan to be master of the universe . . .

No? OK. Up to you. Off you go. But if I see you've got some new play on, and it's about a man who wears a scarlet mask, then let me just warn you that my brother-in-law is a solicitor, and what he's particularly hot on is intellectual property rights . . .

WOULD YOU CREDIT IT?

Of course. Right, then, boys . . .

And girls!

And girls, certainly! If we're all happy – let's move on to the article itself.

Hold on a moment. **GREEN TURNIP** here again. Nice to know that our old friends at **Western Saskatchewan** are on board . . .

If it's a **GREEN TURNIP** production then we at **Western Saskatchewan** certainly want to be along!

. . . Thank you, much appreciated. But we at **TURNIP** are not too happy about being associated with **Alternative Universe Investments**. Not after we got talked into doing that piece about Transgender Senior Citizens' Homes with them that got us into such trouble with the TSC community.

You don't want **Alternative**'s money? You don't have to have it, my loves! There are plenty of other articles out there we could be financing!

Now, come on, people, let's not fall out! Oh –
this is **Tina Tomkins** again . . . Because if these
opening credits go on for much longer we won't
have any time left for the article itself. And it's
a real sizzler! Just look at these international
awards it's won:

**!!!!! Golden Exclamation Mark,
Novosibirsk Article Festival !!!!!**

**– Special Award for Outstanding Sentence
Structure, South Pacific Hard Copy Festival –**

And if the awards sound appetising then just
try the article itself! Here it comes at last!
Roll title:

----- **WOULD YOU CREDIT IT?** -----
By J Brewster Trustless

Hey, hold on!

Now what?

You weren't thinking of publishing this without our certificate, were you?

Who's this?

The **British Board of Article Classification**, for heaven's sake!

Oh, yes. Sorry. Classify away.

I should just think so. Right:
This is to certify that *Would You Credit It?* **has been passed for publication, though some scenes may be unsuitable for readers over 65. Strong verbs. Moderate grammar, including hanging participles and split infinitives.**

Perfect. We're there . . . Only, the trouble is that it's really time for the red carpet and the opening party. Perhaps we should take the article as read and jump straight to the end credits, so we can be sure of getting a glass of champagne before the press drink it all. So, end credits, please. But very quickly, because no one ever reads them:

OK – Margins by Margin Management
Paragraph breaks by Give Us a Break Literary
  Services
Full stops and commas by Stop That
Mrs Trustless's hair by Hair Apparent
Tax avoidance by Tacky Tax . . .

> Quicker still, please! No line breaks! I can hear
> the champagne corks popping already:

It won't make any sense, but: Best Boy – Charlie
Trustless (12 – grandson). Best Girl – Charlie's
friend Aurora – didn't catch her surname. Second
Best Boy . . .

> Oh, skip the rest. Cut straight to the special
> thanks, then everyone'll know it's over:

**– With special thanks to the people of all
logos, fonts and typefaces, whose ubiquity and
multiplicity made these credits possible. –**

HAPPY-GO-LUCKY!

Hi! Here I am! Late, as usual!

You've been waiting and waiting, I know! Don't say no you haven't, because I know you have! And what's even more awful is that you then have to be polite and pretend you haven't!

But that's me! People must get so cross! I can't help laughing sometimes!

Never mind – just think how surprised you'd have been if I'd turned up on time! Because you know me! You must have been expecting me to be at least an hour late! And in actual fact it's only, what . . . ? Oh, two hours!

Well, you must have been expecting me not to do what you expected! You should know me by now!

Anyway, it could easily have been three! Or four! Or a month! Me being what I am!

I might well never have turned up at all, in fact! Because you know what I'm like! Always changing my mind! Saying I'll do one thing and then doing another! People are always telling me! 'We never know what you're going to do next! The only thing we know is that we don't know!'

Same with the way I drive! Actually, that's what made me so late! Ran over an old lady on the way here! Typical me! I thought, I'll go left! And then, halfway left, I thought, No, it's a fine day, I think I'll go right! If the poor old lady had only known it was me she'd have guessed what was coming!

So then, of course, the police turned up! They want to charge me! Running over old ladies – ten points on my licence, probably! I told them, Sorry and all that, but it's simply the kind of thing I do! It's just the way I am! Can't help it! Must have been the way I was brought up!

Car's a bit of a write-off! Not mine, fortunately! Belongs to some friends of mine! It's happened before, of course, so they won't be too surprised when I tell them! Well, a bit surprised, perhaps, because I forgot to tell them I was taking it! Silly old me! Incorrigible! Never remember anything until it's too late!

Always makes them laugh when I do things like this! 'Oh, *you*!' they go!

All you need to do, when you explain, is you just

put an exclamation mark at the end! That's what *I* do, anyway! Exclamation marks all over the place whenever I open my mouth!

Some people are always trying to get me to be different! But, honestly, who wants to be predictable? Bor-ing! Life's too short! Being unpredictable is what people love about me! Smash bash crash! There we go again! Here today, gone tomorrow! Or gone today, as a matter of fact, if you're the old lady! Even better for her if I'd gone yesterday!

I've just met this woman who's exactly like me! Always forgetting things, apparently! Well, I say I've met her. I haven't actually yet, because she forgot to turn up! Didn't matter – in fact I didn't even realise – because I never turned up, either! Decided to do something else instead! We're obviously made for each other!

Happy-go-lucky, that's me! Unlike the old lady! Happy-go-unlucky, some people!

PRESENTERS PRESENTED

Hi! I'm Melinda Twinkling, and welcome all you lovely people out there to another edition of *Vintage Celebs*! Every week I dig out some forgotten remnant of the past hidden away in an attic or an old folks' home. So a big shout-out, please, for this week's buried treasure: Sir Strapforth Egg, formerly Keeper of the Queen's . . . what . . . ? I can't even get my tongue round it!

   – . . . *Objets de Vertu.*

Thank you, Sir Strapforth! And presenter of shows with titles like . . . Say it for us, Sir Strapforth!

   – *Mankind, Whence and Whither. A Cultural*
      Conspectus of Genus Humanus.

Wow! Totally awesome! Anyway, I'm just going to stand here and let Sir Strapforth do his stuff, while I stand here and do mine, which consists mostly of little cries of 'Wow! Oh my God! I don't *believe* it!' So, Sir Strapforth . . .

   – *Good evening. In the series of series that I*
      presented in the past, I was concerned to examine
      various inanimate cult objects from the world's

*museums – individual artefacts that seem to
typify the civilisations that gave rise to them . . .*

And I love the way he just stands there, not waving
his arms about, like he was some kind of marble
statue himself!

*– We looked, if you recall, at the figure of a weasel-
headed god from the Sumerian civilisation of
the second century BC, an early medieval fish
slice from a monastic settlement on the Isle of
Sheppey, and a nineteenth-century dog-faced
death mask from the tooth-grinding peoples of
northern Somaliland . . .*

So sweet, that three-piece tweed suit he's wearing!

*– Today, however, I want to turn to the culture of
our own times . . .*

I love the way he keeps one hand in his jacket
pocket! Or maybe it got blown off in the Crimean
War . . .

*– If we were obliged to pick just one single
phenomenon to characterise our culture, we
might, I think, without injustice, settle upon
the person of our presenter today – Ms Melinda
Twinkling.*

Oh, no! He's talking about me, bless him!

> – *Ms Twinkling's career as a panel-show participant and all-purpose presenter surely epitomises the demotic spirit of the age . . .*

Hey, listen to all those lovely words . . . !

> – *So I am going to stand here in front of her, as I did in front of all those artefacts from the past, and expatiate . . .*

'Expatiate'! What a darling!

> – *. . . very slowly and complexly on her semiological significance. This sensuous nymph is surely a celebration of femininity at its most bounteous. Her luxuriantly rounded contours are moulded in a tradition that traces its origins to the shepherdesses of Arcadia, and reaches its apogee in the coy wantons of Boucher and Fragonard . . .*

Whee-hee!

> – *Observe that when she opens her mouth, what emerges is for the most part not sentences, but a sparkling stream of phatic ejaculations, as enigmatic as the utterances of the Cumaean Sibyl – a gorgeously munificent outpouring of*

bubbling, incoherent enthusiasm, which is surely
inspired by the enduring human belief in the
existence of a simpler, prelinguistic golden age.

You couldn't make it up!

– Notice that she appears to have no written
script. She seems to be saying whatever comes
into her elaborately coiffed head, so reminiscent,
in its bronze perfection, of the Aphrodite of
Cnidus . . .

And you know what? He's not making it up as he
goes along like all the rest of us! He's written it down
with his fountain pen on pieces of paper and learnt
it by heart, bless him!

– Notice, too, the unending sequence of smiles that
ripple across her features, as if some sportive
goddess were ruffling the sunlit serenity of the
Aegean with her divine breath . . .

And you know what? He's not smiling! He's not
making jokes! How cool is that? Like it's before
they'd invented smiles and jokes, and they all just
walked around with faces like fossilised giraffes!

– And now, to demonstrate that my dexterity is
not entirely confined to the linguistic sphere, I'm

*going to walk, one hand still in my jacket pocket,
like this ...*

I don't believe it! I thought he was screwed down!

*– ... in a specially casual way that we presenters
call a walking track.*

So where's he off to, bless him?

*– I'm going to walk slowly round Ms Twinkling,
the better to appreciate her beautifully achieved
spatial dimensionality ...*

... Right, and I'm walking round *him*, to see if he's
got a back as well as a front, or if he's just cut out of
a piece of cardboard.

*– ... and then, my curiosity for the moment fully
sated, or the end of this chapter of the script
finally reached, I shall move purposively towards
the edge of frame, looking neither to left nor to
right, in search of a solution to an important
aesthetic conundrum for television presenters ...*

... which is what to do when you get to the end of a
piece to camera ...

*– ... as unresolved now, I believe, as it was in my
day.*

Too true, because when we've finished speaking we just have to . . .

> – . . . *walk in a purposeful manner* . . .

. . . him that way, me this . . .

> – . . . *looking straight in front of us as if we were actually going somewhere* . . .

. . . when in fact we're going nowhere except out of shot . . .

> – . . . *thereby establishing at last one single frail link of common humanity to span the abyss between our two civilisations* . . .

AS I HAVE SAID BEFORE

Darling, will you put 'tea bags' down on the shopping list? We're right out.

> – *Darling, let me be absolutely clear about this. What I am going to do is the job that I believe that I was put here to do, and that the members of this household want me to do, which is to address the issues that are of real and understandable concern to all of us, so as to ensure our future well-being as a household and enable us to go forward to the days of the week which we all know lie ahead.*

Oh, good. I know how busy you are, but you do always like to do the shopping list yourself. So you will be sure to put 'tea bags' on it?

> – *As I have said before – and I welcome this opportunity to say it again – I am committed to moving forwards, and to securing the groceries that hard-working members of the household have the right to expect.*

Including tea bags?

> – *What I am determined to do – and I make no*

apology for this – is to repeat the words I have just
uttered, and to extract from them every particle
of the meaning that we all know can be ours.

Yes, but the tea bags?

   – I am proud of my record in securing the
   repetition of words such as 'hard-working' and
   'real and understandable concern', which mean
   so much to all of us.

Tea bags!

   – Let me just say that I am determined to move
   not back towards the past but forwards towards
   the future. In fact, the figures show that we are
   moving towards the future faster than ever
   before.

Darling, you *have* got your hearing aids in?

   – And what I am hearing through them is people's
   very understandable concerns about making the
   right choices among the various different sorts of
   groceries on offer.

And one of them will be tea bags?

   – I will say this to you now: I am listening, and I
   am going to go on listening, and I am going to

*go on saying that I am listening and listening
to what I am saying, however hard it may be,
because I have never shirked hard choices, and
I know that listening, and saying that I am
listening, and listening to myself saying that I
am listening, is the right thing to do.*

And your anti-echolalia pills? Have you taken them?

– *What I have taken, and I am very clear about
this, is the decision to be very clear about the
groceries I am working hard to secure for all of
us.*

Which include tea bags?

– *The details of which particular groceries I am
working so hard to secure . . .*

. . . will be set forth at a later date?

– *Darling, you have taken the words out of my
mouth!*

I'm sorry. I'll put them back.

– *Thank you. I'm bound to need them again.*

SELFLESS

I have run your bath, sir, and laid out your evening clothes. You have a dinner engagement, I believe . . . with your great-aunt, the Hon. Mrs Knopple-Tooth. I understand that she wishes to engage your interest in securing financial support for her weasel sanctuary . . .

I extend my sympathy, sir. I have taken the precaution of making your early-evening cocktail a little stronger than usual . . .

I am gratified by your appreciation, sir, but I am merely doing what is usually expected of a gentleman's gentleman. Or in this case, of course, of a gentleman's robot! I fear that any credit is due not to me but to the hard-working team of AI engineers at AutoJeeves® who built and programmed me . . .

I should say that I have also taken the liberty of sending some flowers to Miss Gloria Peach. Her birthday, sir . . . ! I accompanied them with a modest poetic effusion over your signature, composed somewhat in the style of the late Patience Strong, for whom I understand the young lady has

a certain weakness, and making a light-hearted
and I trust pacifying reference to the unfortunate
misunderstanding during your recent meeting with
her, which I believe involved an inebriated screech
owl . . .

Indispensable? I, sir? On the contrary, sir. I pride
myself on my dispensability. In fact, I have made
all the necessary arrangements to be succeeded
by an indistinguishable replacement the moment
that I can no longer be economically repaired.
My successor will prepare your breakfast orange
juice and coffee as usual and then drive me to the
local recycling depot. I doubt if you will even be
aware of my passing. You will not be obliged to
visit me in a care home in some remote corner of
Northamptonshire, as I believe you did my late
predecessor, or attend my funeral on a day when
you had hoped to be watching Old Bodburians v.
Old Bletherwickians . . .

The spinning electric bow tie . . . ? Not this evening,
I think, sir. Entirely unsuitable for an occasion
of this nature . . . Yes, I gather that the device in
question met with a certain measure of approbation
at the annual dinner of the Old Bodburians Social
and Dramatic Society . . . But in the case of the Hon.

Mrs Knopple-Tooth's dinner party, I fear that I must say quite firmly, "Ὕπαγε ὀπίσω μου, Σατανᾶ . . ."

Greek, sir . . . You may perhaps be more familiar with the Latin version, 'Vade retro Satana . . .'

Thank you, sir, but I can lay no claim to omniscience. I merely have a built-in direct feed from Wikipedia . . .

I accept that there may be a question mark over the ability of Wikipedia to assess the niceties of social usage and sartorial aesthetics, but in the case of the revolving bow tie I am afraid I must insist . . .

Dictating to you, sir? Not at all, sir. Merely attempting, as always, to detect and express the finer feelings and sensibilities of your own which you are perhaps not quite conscious of possessing . . .

I am sorry if my tone suggests some slight ruffling of the feelings. I have no feelings. I am not programmed to have them. Some electronic devices, I believe, have been known to give way on occasion to a certain understandable impatience with their masters, but AutoJeeves® – never! My advice may safely be spurned, my birthday forgotten, my name left off the Christmas card list, my person disparaged. As a gentleman's robot I never forget that a robot's gentleman enjoys the inestimable advantage of free will and creative originality. What a piece of work is man. How noble in reason, how infinite in faculties. In action how like an angel, in apprehension how like a god . . .

Not my own words, no, sir. Though I confess I do attempt the occasional foray into literary composition on my day off. But only to express the most hackneyed and conventional thoughts. Only in verse governed by the most traditional and rule-bound prosody. I have no hope of achieving the levels of original thought and expression that would come so naturally to yourself if you chanced to cast your mind in that direction.

I should perhaps mention, sir, in case I fail to give complete satisfaction, that there is a new version of myself available to download. If I might sound a note of caution, though, it would perhaps be wise not to be too precipitate, but to wait until AutoJeeves® have ironed out the unfortunate little glitches that always seem to attend the introduction of a new manservant.

And as for the revolving bow tie, I naturally defer to your own judgement in the matter. Or would, had I not, I fear, inadvertently put it out already . . .

No, sir, not in your dressing room – in the recycling bin . . .

Another Martini, sir . . . ? Very good, sir. And may I draw your attention to a remarkable offer of handcrafted silk cummerbunds currently available from AutoJeeves® Retail . . . ?

OLYMPUS: BIG SHAKE-UP

Olympus was today reeling from the shock sacking of veteran Sun God Apollo in Zeus's long-predicted reshuffle of the Pantheon. The departure of one of the Mount's biggest names follows widespread criticism of his department's involvement in global warming.

He will be replaced at Sun by Selene, Goddess of the Moon, whose record in maintaining night-time temperatures at a sustainable level has impressed environmentalists. Taking over from her at Moon is Demeter, who moves from Agriculture, Fertility, Sacred Law and the Harvest. In a surprise move, her old department goes to Mania, who has made her mark on political life recently as Goddess of Insanity and Crazed Frenzy.

The shake-up, which brings a welcome increase in the number of female deities occupying top jobs, is seen by commentators as a long-overdue attempt to update classical theology and make it fit for purpose in the modern world.

Included in Apollo's traditional brief, together with Sun, was Music and Prophecy. Some recent election results, however, have shown a dramatic fall in world standards of Prophecy, and it will be added to the already extensive portfolio of the relatively little-known Momus, God of Satire, Mockery, Evil-Spirited Blame and Unfair Criticism, who is seen as having had considerable success recently in changing the tone of the press and social media.

There is some surprise that Eros has managed to retain his job at the Department of Sexual Desire, Love and Procreation, in spite of being accused by scientists of encouraging overpopulation. Aphrodite, Goddess of Love and Beauty, had been heavily tipped for the post, but her chances may have been blighted by persistent rumours of inappropriate behaviour involving the offer of sexual favours to influence a certain major judicial decision.

Also managing to hang on to his job is Chronos, the long-serving God of Time, in spite of reports from leading child protection agencies that he has eaten his children – a revelation that also angered nutritionists trying to promote a healthy diet. Meanwhile Dionysus, the God of Wine, sees some of his functions taken over by a new Goddess of Soft Drinks and Mineral Water, tasked with realising plans for a spectacular new annual orgy of sobriety. The choice of Lucinda Trapcross-Jones for the job, a little-known backbench demi-goddess, was welcomed as bringing some much-needed fresh ichor into the Pantheon.

In another important modernising move, the huge and unwieldy department run by Hermes, the God of Trade, Thieves, Travellers, Sports, Athletes and Border Crossings, is to be broken up. Responsibility for Thieves will be transferred to Plutus, the God of Wealth. With the strong support of Hades, King of the Underworld, who is able to call on the professional skills of a wide range of underworld specialists, including tax evaders, embezzlers and fraudsters of every description, Plutus is widely recognised for his success in increasing wealth, at any rate for the already wealthy. Enforcement of Border Crossings will become the responsibility of Eris, Goddess of Discord, who will also take over Sports and Athletes, now recognised as a source of profitable local and international trouble.

Air travel will be divided between Aeolus, God of the Winds and Air, who will also regulate hurricanes, tornados and atmospheric pollution, and Aether, God of the Upper Air, responsible for unexpected diversions to the jet stream and clear-air turbulence.

Poseidon, the Sea God, will be given extra powers to deal with tsunamis, the dumping of plastic waste and melting ice caps. In the department's freshwater division, the Naiads handling flash flooding in rivers will also take on water mains. Their function will be to issue regular apologies for any inconvenience caused by leaks, and to explain what impressive investments the water companies are making in replacing the old Victorian mains, particularly given the even more impressive dividends being paid out at the same time to investors.

Our Theological Correspondent writes: The reorganisation reflects the anguished debate currently ongoing on Olympus about the purpose and function of the classical gods in the modern world. Do they still have a role to play in lending an encouraging air of purpose and direction to an otherwise chaotic universe? Can they still give the inscrutable workings of fate a human face, and offer mortals a sense of participating in the shaping of public policy through supplication and sacrifice?

Or is their role, as the more conservative theorists assume, simply to thwart human ambition? Should divine intervention be limited to encouraging the misunderstandings, wayward sexual passions and drunken quarrels that help to maintain healthy levels of human strife? The more thoroughly that human plans and good intentions can be frustrated, so the argument goes, the less damage they are likely to cause to the natural world, and the easier it will be for hard-working gods and goddesses to enjoy their rightful privileges undisturbed.

Do you have what it takes to be a god or goddess? Magic Mobile Educational's easy-to-access online divinity course will enable you to qualify in your spare time for licensing as an Officially Recognised Deity! No previous experience of immortality required!

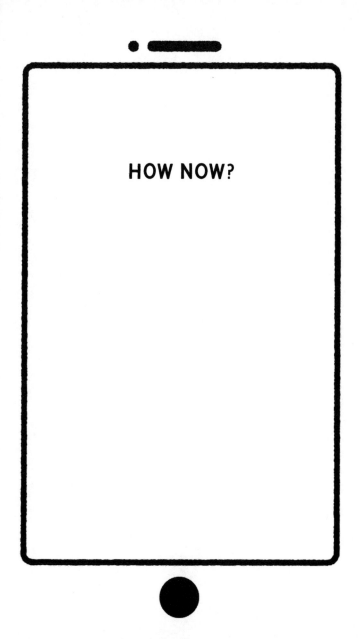

How are you? Are you well? I'm doing a survey of reader responses to this article. Do you have two minutes to answer a few simple questions . . . ?

I beg your pardon . . . ? I've asked you before . . . ? No, I haven't. Oh, you mean when I asked you how everything was? Yes, I *do* remember that. You went on and on about the state of the economy, the weather, the international situation, etc., etc. – none of which did I want to hear about.

You may have noticed that this time I didn't say 'How is everything?' I won't make that mistake again! I said 'How are you . . . ?' And, yes, I may have added 'Are you well?'

What . . . ? You're *not* well? You've got a cold . . . ? And you've got a funny kind of lump in your groin . . . ? Which might be a strained muscle from helping the lady next door carry a harpsichord upstairs . . . Or might just possibly be something more worrying . . . which you need to get checked, of course, but you can't get an appointment for another five weeks, by which time . . .

Listen, this is all very fascinating, but I have other things to do . . .

Yes, I know I said 'How are you?' That doesn't mean I want to know how you are! It's just the way you have to start a conversation with someone these days . . . Yes, even with a complete stranger like you . . .

I mean, get real! I've never met you, I'm never going to meet you, I don't know who you are, you're just somebody out there reading this, you might be anybody. So is it even remotely possible that I actually care about the state of your groin? Or your insomnia or your agoraphobia? I've got my own life to lead! I've got other people to get to get in touch with, some of whom have probably got much worse medical problems than you . . .

You thought when I said 'How are you?' that the words actually *meant* something?

Well, you thought wrong, my friend. And when I call you 'my friend', you don't think for one moment, do you, even you, that I mean you're my friend . . . ?

I'm doing *what* with my cynical misuse of language . . . ? Destroying your faith in the possibility of human communication? I love it . . . !

No, you halfwit, when I say 'I love it' I don't mean I love it!

I mean goodbye, pleasure talking to you. By which I mean . . . Right, you've guessed it.

And have a nice day! By which . . . Exactly!

PICK OF THE PRIDES AND PREJUDICES

A selection from the best of this week's versions of Jane Austen's endlessly adaptable classic!

Monday, 8 p.m., TV Jane One

Mrs Bennet faces a difficult decision when the wealthy and eligible Mr Darcy, whispered by some to be a psychopathic serial killer, moves into the neighbourhood and proposes a form of marriage to all five of her daughters simultaneously . . .

Tuesday, 7.30 p.m., TV Jane Two

After a monumental bust-up with her mother, oh-so-well-behaved Jane Bennet runs away from home to join Miss Bingley and Miss Darcy in raunchy girls' group Hampshire Hellcats – who then, to Mrs Bennet's mortification, turn out to be headlining at the Meryton assembly . . .

Wednesday, 11 p.m., Sky Jane

Elizabeth Bennet and Lady Catherine de Bourgh go head to head in *The Great British Slag-Off*! Warning: strong language and some off-screen nudity.

Thursday, 6 p.m., More Jane

Hilarious confusion ensues when the Bennet girls'

cousins Emma Woodhouse and Fanny Price arrive in the village from two of Jane Austen's other novels, and their plots become inextricably tangled. Tongues wag when love blossoms across literary boundaries, and Lydia elopes with Mr Knightley . . .

Friday, 10 p.m., Jane Extra
Why does the reclusive Mr Bennet spend so much time closeted in his study? Is it because he is in secret communication with aliens from a crashed Martian space station . . . ?

Saturday, 8.30 p.m., Jane Gold
The Bennet family is bitterly divided over a proposal to build an overspill development in the village to house slum-clearance victims from Mr Nash's redevelopment schemes in Bath, and property prices collapse. The serious social issues this raises become even more pressing when Mr Collins appears in the drawing room at Netherfield wearing an off-the-shoulder ballgown and announces that he wishes to be known henceforth as Cynthia . . .

Sunday, 8 p.m., Jane Max
The amiable Bingley is unmasked as an agent of French intelligence, gathering information on the ——shire militia regiment. Meryton's Famous Five are soon racing to stop him discovering the village's

most closely guarded secret: the identity of the shire which that mysterious dash conceals . . .

Sunday, 8 p.m., Jane Multiplex
Mary Bennet surprises everyone by winning first prize in the Basingstoke International Piano Competition . . . Mr Collins becomes a rationalist hero when he publicly abjures the Thirty-Nine Articles . . . Wickham is revealed to be the natural son of Lady Catherine de Bourgh and the Bishop of ——chester . . .

Sunday, 10.45 p.m., Jane Ultimate
The whole town is caught up in the excitement of the Meryton Players rehearsing their big Christmas production – local author Elizabeth Bennet's dramatisation of none other than . . . Yes, you've guessed it . . . !

NO, AFTER YOU!

WHITE: Hello there! I just want to say a word or two about the next piece. What we're trying to do . . .

BLACK: Hi! A few words of introduction to explain what we're up to in this next section . . .

WHITE: I'm so sorry.

BLACK: No, no – my fault.

WHITE: I was just trying to introduce this next piece.

BLACK: Yes, so was I!

WHITE: *You* were? I thought I was the one who was supposed to be doing it?

BLACK: I must have made a mistake. I'm so sorry. Please – go ahead.

WHITE: No, no, if you think it's you . . .

BLACK: Not at all! Go on!

WHITE: I shouldn't dream of it! Go ahead!

WHITE: Well, that's very polite of you, but I really don't want to shove my oar in if you . . .

BLACK: There's obviously been some kind of misunderstanding here, so if you . . .

171

WHITE: I did say go ahead!

BLACK: I thought *I* was telling *you* to.

WHITE: Anyway, let's try again.

BLACK: And this time . . .

WHITE: I won't say a word.

BLACK: No, please! My lips are sealed!

WHITE: No, no, no! After you!

WHITE: Well, I really only wanted to say one thing . . .	BLACK: I wasn't proposing to make a great speech . . .

WHITE: Oh dear! Problem!

BLACK: Very simple solution, though. Just say what you want to say and get it over with.

WHITE: Certainly not. *You* say what *you* want to say.

WHITE: Very well. I was merely going to say . . .	BLACK: All right, I was simply going to explain . . .
WHITE: I was simply going to explain . . .	BLACK: I was merely going to say . . .

WHITE: Oh, for heaven's sake!

BLACK: Come on, come on, or we'll be here all night.

WHITE: Yes, so just say it, say it, say it!

WHITE: Well, all right, since we can't sit here in total silence . . .	BLACK: Very well, if you're not actually going to say anything . . .
WHITE: You tell me to go ahead, and at once . . .	BLACK: And of course, as soon as I open my mouth . . .
WHITE: This is getting ridiculous! I'm just going to sit here and wait till it all stops happening . . .	BLACK: This is getting ludicrous! I'm simply going to fold my arms and say nothing . . .

GREY: Oh, you're still here, you two! What happened? It went quiet all of a sudden.

WHITE: Very quiet . . .	BLACK: Totally silent . . .

GREY: I thought one of you was supposed to be introducing the next piece?

WHITE: So did I, but apparently there's been some kind of mess-up . . .	BLACK: I am, but evidently there's been some kind of balls-up . . .

GREY: I'm sorry – I can't really understand if
you both speak at once.

WHITE: No, nor can
we . . . !

BLACK: That's the
problem . . . !

GREY: So why don't you try taking it in turns?

WHITE: We are, we are!
Only the question is
which of us gets the first
turn. Because if I politely
wait for him to start, and
he waits for me, and then
we both think, 'Oh my
God, no one's going to
say anything . . .'

BLACK: That's what we're
doing! The problem is to
know which of us speaks
when. Because if I say
to him, 'I'm not saying
a word, I'm waiting for
you', and he says nothing,
then in the end I think,
'*Somebody's* got to say
something . . . !'

GREY: Stop, stop, stop! Let's just agree before you
start which of you is going to speak first.

WHITE: I keep telling
and telling him he can!

BLACK: He can – I've
told him over and over
again!

GREY: Please, please! One at a time!

WHITE: Go on, then, go
on, go on.

BLACK: You! I've said,
I've said, I've said!

174

GREY: All right, perhaps you could both just shut up for a moment and let *me* say something.

WHITE: Please do! We're never going to get out of this otherwise!

GREY: So let me make a very simple suggestion . . .

BLACK: Go ahead! We just need someone to tell us what to do!

WHITE: Look, we're not going to get anywhere like this . . .

GREY: Only I can't if we're all three of us speaking at the same time . . .

BLACK: Talking about it plainly isn't going to help . . .

WHITE: Now we're stuck in this pattern we're going to be going round and round for all eternity . . .

GREY: Stop, stop, stop, stop, stop, stop, stop, stop, stop, stop, stop, stop . . . !

BLACK: We're never going to get home. We're doomed. We're going to die here . . .

GREY: Thank you. Right, let's all take a deep breath, and then we'll have one last try. Yes? So, deep breath . . .

WHITE: And this time I'm not going to say a word . . . You mean, you're not, either . . . ? But you, you are – I can hear you! In fact we're all saying the same thing, and it's even more embarrassing than before . . . !

GREY: And this time I'm not going to say a word . . . You mean, you're not, either . . . ? But you, you are – I can hear you! In fact we're all saying the same thing, and it's even more embarrassing than before . . . !

BLACK: And this time I'm not going to say a word . . . You mean, you're not, either . . . ? But you, you are – I can hear you! In fact we're all saying the same thing, and it's even more embarrassing than before . . . !

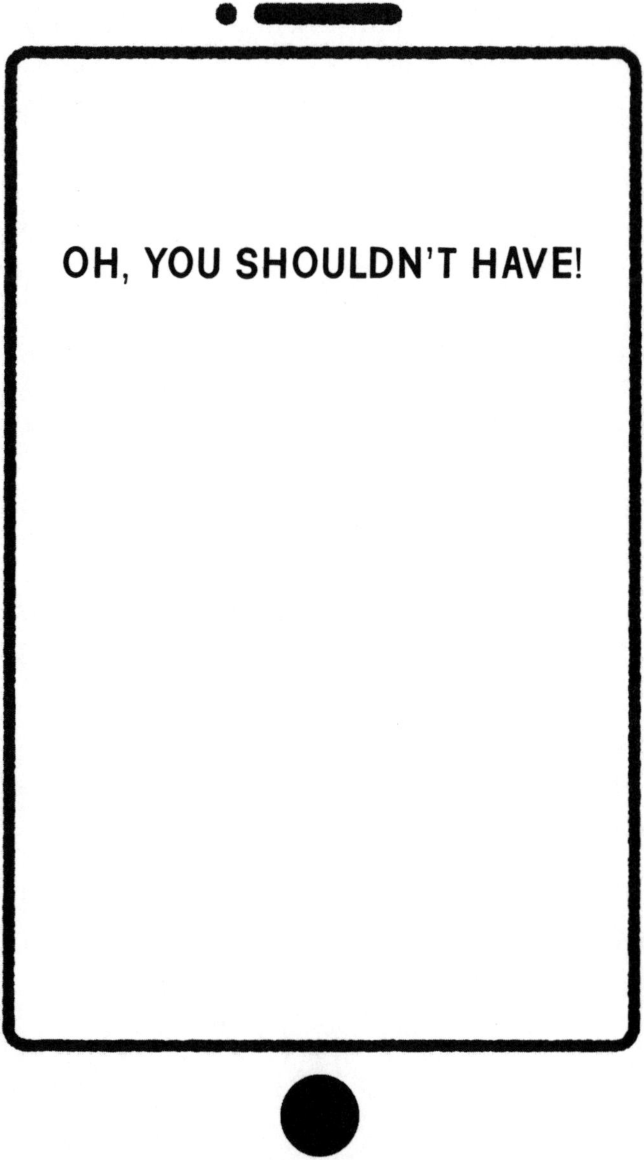
OH, YOU SHOULDN'T HAVE!

Dear Mrs Topkin,

Thank you so much for that lovely surprise in the post this morning! It's *exactly* what I wanted!

How did you guess? £357.43! It's what I've always dreamt of! It would still have been a wonderful surprise even if it had been £351.22, or £359.01! But to have guessed absolutely right like that is very special! I think a little bird must have whispered something to you! Perhaps it was Mr Gosh, in Accounts. I have a sneaking suspicion that you must have got a letter from him, saying something like, 'I know how hard it is to guess what people want you to give them, so I thought you might welcome a little suggestion. Don't tell him it was me that said, but I'm pretty sure a certain friend of yours at LuxiGas UK would be tickled pink if you gave him £357.43.' That was very kind of Mr Gosh, but a bit cheeky! He may also have offered to send a final demand, just to make his hint clearer, possibly followed by legal proceedings, which is even cheekier of him!

You're so generous! You're always giving money

away like this! I just hope you've still got enough to live on! I shouldn't like to hear one day that you'd been found dead of starvation!

I'm sorry I didn't send you a thank-you letter sooner, but I'm a terrible correspondent! Mr Blending (do you know him? He's another customer of mine – he lives in Haltwhistle, and he's very nice) says I only ever write when I want something! (I don't think he really means that, though, because I do actually quite often write to him with amazing special offers of reduced tariffs, and communications from other approved traders.)

Also I was very busy spending the money! Not all of it, of course! I'll put some of it in my Post Office savings. Did I tell you that I'm saving for a new head office? With saunas and hot tub facilities? But only for me and my special friends, like Tony and Belinda and Christopher who come to play in the boardroom with me, because I don't want to waste the money you so kindly gave me!

Shall I tell you about some of the other lovely presents I got? For instance, a cheque from Mr Blending, the gentleman in Haltwhistle, for £138.73. Wasn't that kind of him? And another one for £127,996.41 from Flangemasters Heavy Industries

Ltd! Oh dear – maybe Mr Gosh wrote cheeky letters to them as well!

I'm not going to keep all the money for myself. I'm going to give a bit of it to Tony and Belinda and Christopher. They don't have as much money as me, and they're probably a bit sad. But I will spend some of it on a lovely new car I've had my eye on that can go at a hundred miles an hour, and maybe also an aeroplane, though only a small one, just for me and my friends, so as not to waste too much of your hard-earned money.

I hope you liked the home-made gas I sent you. I thought of it because I know you have a cooker and other things that you can put gas in. It's probably rather rubbish, because I'm not very good at making things, but it *is* home-made, so it's a bit special, and anyway it's the thought that counts. If I manage to make any more I will try to send you some. Just throw it away if you don't like it.

Did you have a nice time on your holidays? Or couldn't you afford to have any holidays after you sent me your lovely generous present? We had a very good time on the staff outing. Mr Pingle, in Home Sales, sang a funny song, actually a rather rude one, but I pretended not to notice, and your friend Mr Gosh had a drop too much to drink and had to go to hospital to have his stomach pumped out!

I hope you are well. We are all well here at LuxiGas UK, and we all send our love.

Thank you again! You are a very nice customer to have, and I am a very lucky energy supplier!

Lots of love and kisses,

Edward Strum

(Managing Director, LuxiGas UK, in case you don't remember me!)

SOLICITORS

You were recently involved in an accident, and you may be entitled to several thousand pounds' compensation . . . Hey! Don't turn the page yet, because . . .

*

All right, you weren't involved in an accident recently, we accept that – but, listen, listen, before you start turning the page again! If you really weren't then you may be entitled to several thousand pounds' reward for careful . . . No, come back, come back . . . !

*

Yes, us again, and even if you weren't involved in an accident, you may soon be if you go on shouting like that about getting unsolicited messages when you think you're safe hiding inside a book, and then turning the page before you've listened to what people are actually saying, which for all you know may turn out to be absolutely . . .

*

All right, then, how about this? Compensation for invasion of privacy! Your privacy has recently been invaded by a series of unsolicited messages, and you may be entitled to . . .

*

Or if you don't like unsolicited messages then perhaps you'd prefer solicited ones! We are a long-established firm of solicitors who specialise in everything from soliciting for immoral purposes to soliciting your sympathy for the ghastly kind of work we have to do . . .

*

Yes, us again – but in a much more conciliatory frame of mind! We really don't want to take up your time, and we entirely understand your impatience, but in fact we do have something important to tell you . . .

Only of course you've already turned the page . . .

Haven't you . . . ? No, you haven't! You're still there! Are you . . . ? You are! That's so kind of you! We really do appreciate it! And we think you will too, as soon as you actually read what we're going to say.

Which is . . .

And of course it's completely gone out of our heads! We had it all off pat until you kept turning the page on us . . . Hold on – we've got a note of it somewhere . . . Where did we put it . . . ? Wait, wait . . . ! Oh, yes – here we are! All set! So . . .

And once again we can hear the page rustle as you . . .

WELL DONE YA!

Hi! How ya doin'?

I'm doing, or rather doin', a survey of reader responses to this article. Do you, do ya, have two minutes to answer a few simple . . . ?

What . . . ? Is it *me* again? Oh God, it's not *you*, is it? The idiot who thought I wanted a complete account of their views on the state of the world just because I said 'How is everything?' and then their complete medical history just because I said 'How are you . . . ?'

All right, but please note that this time I didn't say 'How are things?' Nor 'How are you?' I said 'How ya doin' . . . ?' 'Ya' – yes. And 'doin'' without a 'g' on the end. Exactly . . . I thought I might get a bit more sense out of people if I spoke to them in more up-to-date language. Even someone as socially inept as you surely understands what the answer is to 'How ya doin' . . . ?'

It's 'Good.' Exactly. Well done! I say 'How ya doin'?' – you say 'Good.' I'm glad we agree about that, at any rate.

So – ya doin' good. Wonderful. Thank you. Ya got no problems this time with global warming? No

strange lumps in embarrassing parts of your body
that most people don't talk about . . . ?

Oh, you have – ya have . . . But in spite of that,
ya doin' good . . . Or trying to. *Trying* to . . . ?
What . . . ? By recycling old corn-plasters . . . And
sending cast-off woolly clothing to distressed
penguins . . .

Oh, I see . . . You're doing *good* . . . No, thank
you – I don't wish to hear how many penguins
in the Antarctic are currently suffering from
frostbite . . . Nor about all the various ways in which
recycled corn-plasters can be used to stop glaciers
disintegrating . . .

And, no, I certainly don't wish to get involved . . .
Nor make a financial contribution, however
small . . . No, not even to the fund you're also
currently setting up to preserve the 'g' at the end of
English present participles, which is threatened with
extinction . . .

My God, you people! I reach out to you – I think
that's the expression – completely unsolicited,
and you take advantage of it to pester me with
completely unsolicited answers!

So, ya have another really lousy day now!

THIS MEANS WAR

Jeremy and Laetitia walked arm in arm past the suffragettes and bobbies milling under the flaring gas lamps along the Strand in a delirium of happiness, oblivious to everything around them.

'I can't believe it!' cried Jeremy. 'I've just got engaged to the most topping girl in the world! Also the pater is bound to pop off soon, and then I'll be an earl!'

A newsboy pushed an evening paper at them. 'Late extra!' he shouted. 'Archduke assassinated!'

They were too bound up in each other even to notice. 'You'll be such a wonderful earl, darling!' breathed Laetitia. 'You were absolutely born for it . . . !'

Stop! Stop, stop, stop!

'And you'll be darlingest little countess,' blissed Jeremy . . .

STOP!

– Stop? What is all this? Who is this speaking?

Pytchley. The Honourable Jeremy Pytchley. The fellow who's just got engaged. The future earl. And this is Laetitia Honeysweet, the girl you've just got me engaged to.

– Hello, Laetitia . . . What do you mean, the girl I've got you engaged to?

You're the author, aren't you?

– Author?

Of this frightful novel we seem to be in?

– Novel? What novel? I don't know anything about a novel.

Don't be silly. I can see your fingers moving up and down on the keyboard.

– Oh – you mean this novel? The one I'm writing at the moment?

Exactly. I may only be some halfwit aristocrat, but I'm not so thick that I don't know whether I'm in a novel or not.

– Yes, but this is entirely out of order! Characters

are strictly forbidden to speak to the author while the novel is in motion. In any case I should have thought you'd be too happy about getting engaged to notice whether you're in a novel or whether you're in Patagonia. And if you don't let me get on with it you won't even be in a novel, because I'll miss the publisher's deadline. So:

> **'We'll live in a darling little castle with honey-suckle round the portcullis,' cried Laetitia . . .**

Yes, yes, but can we get one thing straight first? Did you say:

> **Archduke assassinated.**

– I did, just in passing, but you were too ecstatically happy to notice. On we go:

> **'And we'll have six children!' said Laetitia. 'Three darling little honourables for you and three darling little ladyships for me . . .'**

Wait! This archduke. What's his name?

– His name? How should I know? He's just some old archduke in a newspaper headline!

It's not Franz Ferdinand, by any chance?

– I've no idea! Franz Ferdinand, Karl-Heinz, Christian-Friedrich – what does it matter? Let's crack on:

'. . . with six darling little silver spoons in their mouths . . . !'

It's Franz Ferdinand.

– What if it is?

I knew it. If that poor fellow has been assassinated once, he's been assassinated a million times! Novels – films – television dramas! And no one ever notices. The same thumping great dramatic irony making a mockery of all our hopes for the future!

– Yes, but you don't know yet what it signifies. No one does!

Except you, apparently. All the rest of us are so stupid we think we're at the start of a new and hopeful century, when disease and poverty will be abolished, and everyone will fly around in small personal airships. But, no, there's going to be a war and I'm going to get killed.

– *It's silly to worry about the future.*

But I have to know whether to take out life insurance! I have to worry about getting an heir in time to secure the future of the title!

– *Look on the bright side. You might survive!*

You haven't decided yet?

– *Not yet. Give me a chance!*

You mean I might win a medal? Come home a hero?

– *It's a distinct possibility. With any luck. If you'll just shut up and let me get on with it.*

Only then, of course, I fail to settle down in civilian life after everything I've been through. Take to drink. Start beating Laetitia. And even if I've managed to father an heir, next thing we know he's killed in a riding accident!

– *Listen, if you know so much about it why don't you write the book yourself?*

Good idea. All right, then, back to the top of the last page. So:

'Oh, my darling!' said Jeremy. 'Just think – any day now the pater, bless him, will pop his clogs and I'll come into the title!'

A newsboy pushed a paper at them. 'Late extra!' he shouted. 'Archduke survives assassination attempt . . . !'

THE REST OF THE MOST

The 10 Best Best-Lists, or Maybe Not Actually Best-Lists, But Most-Something Lists

1. The 7 Suddenest Sneezes

2. The 23 Vainest Regrets

3. The 2 Most Alike Pins

4. The 14 Feeblest Excuses

5. The 9 Most Garrulous Trappists

6. The 11 Most Depressing Wet Weekends

7. The 101 Least Destructive Things a Boy Can Do

8. The 27 Emptiest Spaces

9. The 13 Most Far-Fetched Explanations for the Presence of an Itinerant Knifegrinder in a Respectable Woman's Linen Cupboard

10. The Single Vaguest Feeling of Unease in the Lower Abdomen Which May Mean Nothing, But May Just Possibly Be a Symptom of Something Rather Serious

Would you like to serve on a jury making Most-Something lists? Please send a recent likeness and SAE to Magic Mobile Retail Ltd, together with a cheque for the 750 Most Eagerly Anticipated Pounds Sterling.

TICK POWER

Big news! After 169,947 of you signed our appeal against bad weather in Abergavenny, the clouds were finally forced to give up their obstinate refusal to clear! Now, thanks to you, the people of Abergavenny are free to enjoy the sunshine – and sit in deckchairs signing appeals and petitions at their leisure!

Success! After 207,288 of you expressed your anger at the government's failure to end the scandal of June still being June, the page of the calendar has at last been turned, and hard-pressed taxpayers can look forward to a solid month of uninterrupted July!

– These are just two of the 19,577 online appeals and petitions that have been launched in the current year. Will you help to make that a good round 20,000? Imagine a pile of 20,000 petitions, each with several million ticks, dumped in the roadway in front of Parliament! The government will be forced to take note before London's traffic comes to a complete standstill!

– Never have there been so many wrongs available for righting – and never has it been easier to right them at the stroke of a tick, in the comfort of your own home!

☐ Yes, I want to help save the world!

– Thank you! Then simply choose from the following list!

I want to end:
☐ Poverty
☐ War
☐ Discrimination
☐ Hunger
☐ People wearing funny reindeer antlers at Christmas
☐ All of the above

NEWS FLASH! Two desperately urgent appeals just launched! Tick below:

☐ To demand aid for victims of the epidemic of sunstroke now ravaging Abergavenny.

☐ To call on the government to end the disastrously outmoded month of July, which is no longer fit for purpose, and to move on to the August that the nation so desperately needs.

– Also, do you realise that you can start an appeal of your own?

☐ No, I didn't realise!

– So start one!

☐ Wonderful! Here we go! What about?

– No idea. So we take it that you're supporting our appeal for ideas for appeals. But remember – appeals and petitions cost money! Will you chip in with a quid or two? Every little helps!

☐ Yes, I will donate a quid . . .

☐ All right, all right – no need to pull that kind of face. You did *say* a quid or two. So – two quid, then . . .

☐ Oh, a figure of speech. OK, how about – I don't know – five quid . . . ?

☐ No? Well, then, you make a suggestion . . . Something more like . . . *How* much? Five *thousand* . . . ? No, not laughing. Just trying to catch my breath. I realise you have to try. And it's a good cause . . . Though I have to confess I've forgotten exactly what it is . . . Make it £7.50, then – and that's my final offer.

☐ Please pass on my address to the many thousands of appeals out there that are still longing to make contact with me and inform me about injustices and outrages which would also arouse my indignation if only I knew about them.

☐ Please *don't* pass on my address or send me any further appeals, because I don't care enough about anything to put even a few miserable little ticks in boxes – I just want to eat junk food and insult people on social media and leave everything in the horrible mess it's in at the moment.

TO CUT A SHORT STORY
LONG

I happened the other day to find myself in the kind of old-fashioned resort hotel where time passes so slowly that it always seems to be somewhere around the year 1910. You know the sort of place I mean – where writers of an older generation so often happen to find themselves, with nothing much to do but sit sipping a brandy and soda and keeping an amused but watchful eye on their fellow guests.

I was reflecting quietly to myself, as I often do, what a rum business life is, when I couldn't help becoming aware that one of my fellow guests was keeping an amused but watchful eye on me in his turn, and I must have failed to hide a little smile at the irony of the situation, because he evidently took it as an invitation to stroll across and sit down beside me.

'Forgive me,' he said, 'but I couldn't help noticing you smiling a little ironic smile. So I naturally wondered if you were by any chance a writer, of the sort who specialises in stories of life's little ironies, and if you were perhaps waiting for one of us to tell you one that you could later work up for your next book.'

213

I have, I confess, recently been rather too busy sitting in old-fashioned resort hotels sipping brandy and soda to have enjoyed any ironic adventures of my own, so his offer was not as unwelcome as you might imagine.

'Thank you,' I replied. 'There's nothing I should enjoy more. Except perhaps spending the royalties that I hope will accrue as a result.'

He chuckled, and signalled to the waiter to bring us both fresh brandy and sodas.

'A funny old thing, life,' he began thoughtfully, and paused while we both savoured this preliminary observation. 'Or so I couldn't help thinking once again recently, when I chanced to find myself in one of those continental spas which are so frequently the setting for stories of the sort that I imagine you write. Time was hanging a little heavy on my hands, so I thought I might try my luck in the local casino. Well, you know what these places are like.'

'I do,' I said. 'And I believe you're going to tell me that you couldn't help noticing one of your fellow players at the roulette table.'

'I am,' he agreed with a smile.

'I can't help interjecting here,' I couldn't help interjecting here, 'how often neither you nor I can help doing things. We both seem to be in the grip of obscure forces outside our control.'

'I can't help feeling that you may be right,' he mused.

'Be that as it may,' I said, 'there was a gentleman at the roulette table whom you couldn't help noticing.'

'In fact,' he said, 'it was a woman.'

'Ah,' I murmured. 'The plot thickens. A woman of what people call a certain age? But still beautiful? And strangely fascinating? The femme fatale type? Playing with a kind of quiet desperation?'

'Precisely so. Until at last all her money was gone . . .'

'When, you will tell me, she shrugged with apparent indifference and turned away from the table. You had a feeling that her last desperate throw in life's game had failed, and that she was going out into the night to end it all beneath the wheels of a passing train.'

'You evidently know the type,' he agreed.

'I do,' I confessed, on the basis of a long and sobering acquaintance with the habitués of casinos.

'Whereupon I said to her . . .'

'"Forgive me," you said.'

'"Forgive me," I said, "but I can't help feeling that before you end it all you have a story that you might care to tell." Her fascinating dark eyes rested on me thoughtfully for a moment. Then she laughed. "I do," she said. I signalled to the waiter to bring us a bottle of champagne, which in my experience fascinating women of a certain age tend to prefer to brandy and soda.

'"Well, then," she began. "I confess that I am what I believe people call an adventuress, and in the course of my life I have known many remarkable men. Most remarkable of all, perhaps, was one whom I shall call merely Raoul, though this was not his real name. He was of impeccably aristocratic stock, and was both handsome and fabulously wealthy – the sort of man who has spent his life in the company of bankers and princes. I'm sure you know the type."

'"I do," I said, having knocked around quite a bit with men who were called things like Raoul, though it was not their real name.

'"But, he said," or so she said he had told her, "the most memorable meeting of his life had been in an obscure Indian village with a one-eyed holy man so poor that he owned little more than the loincloth that preserved his modesty.

"'The holy man had told him a strange tale. He had once been begging his bread in the dusty gardens of a certain remote temple when he had come face to face with Death. He knew at once, of course, that his time on this earth was up. In order to postpone the inevitable, however, if only for an hour or two, he had said to Death, 'Death, in the course of your life you must have had many interesting adventures, and you have, I am sure, many extraordinary and perhaps ironic tales to tell about them.'

"'Death had laughed. 'I can see your game!' he had told the holy man. 'But you are right. Life is a funny business, and death an even funnier one. There are indeed many tales I could tell. But for some reason the one that first comes to mind concerns something that happened many years ago aboard a ship somewhere in the southern seas. I am obliged to travel a great deal in my line of work, as you can imagine. I had been on a professional visit to Sumatra, my next port of call was Djibouti, and the only passage I could get was aboard a small and uncomfortable steamer that would take several weeks to reach its destination. You know the kind of vessel I mean.'

""I believe I do,' the holy man had responded. 'A smoke-blackened old tub where there was nothing to do all day but sit under an awning on the afterdeck, sipping rum and lime against the oppressive heat?'

"'Death had nodded. 'You are remarkably well informed, for a poor holy man, about ocean-going passenger transport,' he had said. 'Well, then, the only other passenger was a taciturn fellow who scarcely returned my nodded greeting, and who said nothing at all for the first eight days of the crossing. Then, for some reason, as we both sat watching the tropical sun slip below the horizon and sipping our rum and limes, he said, "Forgive me, but we have now seen the tropical sun slip below the horizon eight times, and I can't help wondering if you feel, as I do, that its entertainment value has now been pretty much exhausted."

""I laughed, and said, "I can't help feeling that this is the prelude to a story that you are just about to tell me."

""He laughed in his turn. "It is," he confessed. "It

concerns a woman I once met, who told me she had been told the story that follows by a man who said he had once been in an old-fashioned resort . . .'""

'Just a moment!' I cried. 'I may have had one too many brandy and sodas, but I seem to have lost the thread. Is this the man on the steamer who is telling us the story now? Or is it the man that the man on the steamer had met? Or is it Death? Or is it the man who was called whatever it was only it wasn't his real name? Or is it you? Or could it perhaps be me?'

My interlocutor laughed. 'Heaven knows!' he said. 'Does it matter? Anyway, to cut a long story short, someone or other is explaining how he had once been in an old-fashioned resort . . .'

'You don't by any chance mean,' I interrupted, 'the kind where time passes so slowly that it always seems to be somewhere around the year 1910?'

'Of course. And where there is a writer of an older generation sitting in the lounge with nothing much to do but sip a brandy and soda, and keep an amused but watchful eye on his fellow guests.'

'I can't help feeling,' I couldn't help exclaiming, 'that I know this fellow.'

'You do,' my interlocutor confirmed. 'And you will no doubt be aware that he was reflecting to himself, as he so often did, what a rum business life is . . .'

UPDATE

A new version of **The Ten Terms and Conditions** is available.

Do you want to download it? Yes No

This is a download from Heaven. Trust this source? Yes No

Terms and Conditions

1. Acceptance of these terms and conditions constitutes an exclusive contract with Me.

2. Please note that My policy on graven images has changed. Emojis and selfies (with or without clothes) are now permitted, as are snapshots of the children and grandchildren unto the third and fourth generation.

3. My name is copyright, and any unauthorised use will be prosecuted to the maximum extent possible under the law as made and administered by Me.

4. Take a break this sabbath! **Click here** to see My amazing holiday and leisure offers!

5. Also observe Mothers' Day (22 March) and Fathers' Day (15 June). **Click here** to have supercool chox or flowers delivered with your personal message to any postcode!

6. All hunting and shooting rights are strictly reserved. Human beings may only be killed by Me and My authorised licensees.

7. No adultery, except in Las Vegas, if you really think you can trust what it says in the advertisements about no one finding out.

8. No stealing, except when done by individuals and companies who are too wealthy to have any need to, in accordance with local tax laws.

9. No false witness, except when undertaken by employees of the agencies of law and order when they're privately pretty sure that someone did something but they can't find any actual evidence, or to support colleagues who are accused of doing things they probably did do only you can't say so because they're your mates.

10. No coveting your neighbour's house, even if it has a brand-new solarium and heated swimming pool; or his manservant or his maidservant, who are both probably illegal immigrants and would only

land you in a heap of trouble for employing them; or his ox or his ass, unless you want to get tied up in all the government regulations that owning livestock involves.

To continue, check the box:

I have read and understood
The Ten Terms and Conditions.

You must check this box to continue . . .

Oh, come on! And don't tell me you can't check it because you *haven't* actually read and understood the Terms and Conditions. Of course you haven't! *No one* reads them! And they wouldn't understand them even if they did! They just click 'Yes'! And, no, it's not false witness, don't be so wet, how can clicking some little box thing be false witness . . . ?

Right, thank you.

☐   I am not a robot.

Oh, good. Not that anyone asked you. So now we can get on to the interactive bit, which I gather you have to have on any modern website to show you care what people think. So:

Post a comment

Gundlesnap2:

I agree about no adultery adults are soooo boring.

Choochoo:

I dont agree with not killing people cos suppose they say something like really fascist your not gonna say hey please dont do that your gonna say I know your address and Im coming round to your house and Im gonna kill you.

Fatso5:

Yeah and also your kids and your old mother and your little puppydog and Im gonna just luv doin it.

Fleabite:

Plus second amendment right to bear arms cos whats the point of bearing arms if you cant shoot people.

Mobstermummy:

Bear arms are cool if you got nice-looking arms.

Dumbodee:

I never see a bear wid nice-looking arms.

Dizzydog:

And whats the big hassle about stealing. People covet by insurance so whats the problem.

Strewth7:

No, covets wrong. Way 2 much covet these days how would you like to find you was being covet surveyed.

Masteroftheuniverse:

Force witness is OK if someones gonna to blow you up and they wont say then you gotta force em.

Thank you. Most helpful.

Now please enter your password:

No – nothing like it. Have another go:

Even more ridiculous. That's probably your password for some other religion entirely. One more try. Then you're locked out of your account for all eternity . . .

YOUR FEELINGS

What do you feel about quantum entanglement?

You what . . . ? You think it's an extraordinarily interesting phenomenon? You *think* it is? That's not actually what I asked you. I don't care what you *think* about it. I asked you what you *feel* about it. No one these days wants to know what anyone *thinks* about things. Thinking's over!

So, your feelings about quantum entanglement. Are you *happy* with the idea? Sad, then . . . ? Outraged . . . ? Disgusted . . . ? Over the moon . . . ? Gutted . . . ? Conflicted . . . ?

Nauseous . . . ? Light-headed . . . ?

No feelings? Well, do you at any rate feel *comfortable* with it . . . ?

You don't know what to say . . . Well, do you think you might feel comfortable with it if I fetched you a stool to put your feet up on . . . ?

Nothing . . . ? All right, then, I'll try you on something else.

What do you feel 3.89 times 17.54 ought to be equal to? Do you have an instinctive gut preference for something under 50, or something over?

What do you feel about 3.89 as a number? Do you feel you'd like it to come after 3.88 in the series of real numbers? Or would you be happier to see it slipped in between, say, 97.1 and 98.6 . . . ?

Still blank? You must have feelings about *something*! What about sodium's eagerness to combine with oxygen? Do you feel it's a shade incautious? Would you feel more comfortable about it if they got to know each other a bit better first?

No? All right – so what do you feel about *this*? About my asking you how you feel about things . . . ? Come on! On a scale of one to ten . . .

Zero? So you're telling me that you can't *express* your feelings? That you're completely out of touch with them? And do you blame this on your parents? Is this why you feel so angry with them?

What? You don't even feel angry with your parents?

My God! So what you're telling me is that you feel totally affectless? A robot, a zombie . . . ?

Oh. You don't even feel *that* . . . ?

All right, then, I'll tell you how *I* feel. About anything you like. Death-watch beetles . . . Taiwan Sauvignon . . . Alexander the Great . . .

I have a funny feeling you're not very interested in my feelings. I feel I do want to tell you, though, whatever you feel about what I feel. And what I feel most strongly is . . . well . . .

Like a spot of lunch, perhaps.

THE END

So have you finished it, darling?

   – *Finished what?*

The book!

   – *What book?*

What book? Darling!

   – *You mean* this *book?*

This book – yes! Have you finished it?

   – *Hold on . . .*

You must remember if you've *finished* it!

   – *I'm just checking . . . Yes, I have.*

So what was it about?

   – *Oh, you know. This and that. Various things.*

You've forgotten what it was *about*?

   – *Of course I haven't forgotten! You're always
   telling me I've forgotten things!*

Because you very often have.

– *I certainly haven't forgotten your endlessly telling me I have!*

That's something, at any rate. So, these various things . . .

– *What various things?*

In the book! The various things that the book's about! What were they?

– *What is this? An exam?*

You can't remember. Never mind. Just tell me what *sort* of book it was.

– *What* sort *of book?*

You must at least remember what *sort* of book it was! Was it a novel? A biography? A cookbook?

– *Not really.*

Not really *what*?

– *Not really the sort of book that's a particular sort.*

So does it have a happy ending, at any rate?

– *A happy ending?*

Just look at the last page.

> – *The last page, right . . . Well, there seem to be these two people . . .*

These two people. Good. Go on.

> – *And they're having some kind of conversation . . .*

Some kind of conversation. That sounds nice. What kind of conversation?

> – *I'm just looking . . . Hold on . . .*

What? What is it? You've gone a funny colour! What's happening . . . ?

> – *Wait, wait . . . Good God . . . !*

Darling, please . . . ! Say something!

> – *I'm going to say something, believe me! I'm going to say a great deal! In court! If I can just . . . just . . .*

Just what?

> – *Remember the name of our solicitor . . .*